SIN

A NEW
UNDERSTANDING
OF VIRTUE
AND VICE

JAMES
TAYLOR

SIN

A NEW
UNDERSTANDING
OF VIRTUE
AND VICE

Northstone

Editor: Michael Schwartzentruber
Cover design: Lois Huey-Heck, Margaret Kyle
Interior design: Margaret Kyle
Consulting art director: Robert MacDonald

Permissions:

Quotations from *Dark Nature* Copyright © Lyall Watson 1995, published by Hodder and Stoughton Limited. Reprinted by permission of Hodder and Stoughton and HarperCollins Publishers.

Northstone Publishing Inc. is an employee-owned company, committed to caring for the environment and all creation. Northstone recycles, reuses and composts, and encourages readers to do the same. Resources are printed on recycled paper and more environmentally friendly groundwood papers (newsprint), whenever possible. The trees used are replaced through donations to the Scoutrees For Canada Program.
Ten percent of all profit is donated to charitable organizations.

Canadian Cataloguing in Publication Data
Taylor, James, 1936–
Sin
Includes bibliographical references.
ISBN 1–896836–00–3
1. Sin. 2. Good and evil. I. Title

BT715.T39 1997   241'.3   C96–910888–5

Published by Northstone Publishing Inc.

Printing
9 8 7 6 5 4 3 2 1

Printed in Canada by
Friesen Printers

Dedication

To my father, Dr. W. S. (Bill) Taylor

CONTENTS

The Experience of Evil

The Seven Deadly Sins

The Nature of Sin

The Theology of Sin

The "So What?" of Sin

The
Experience of
Evil

1

Tearing the Veil

Latent evil lurks much closer to the surface of our comfortable lives than we like to admit.

The veil that separates comfortable life from latent evil is very thin. I realized that one sunny, summer afternoon at Rock Lake – a tiny, clear, pea-green pond in the Canadian Rockies.

Over a water fight, of all things.

Michelle started it. Sanjan ended it.

Michelle was the lifeguard, sunning herself on the dock, while Sanjan, a ten-year-old refugee from Bosnia, drifted on the waters of the lake in a bright red canoe. The only ripples on the water came from a family of loons paddling a safe course out in the middle of the lake, well out of Sanjan's enthusiastic but not always skillful attempts at maneuvering the canoe.

The sun beamed down. The seniors at the camp reclined in their lawn chairs, watching nothing much happen.

Sanjan headed in for shore. I strolled down the sand to give him a hand pulling the canoe up.

Perhaps I heard her footsteps. Perhaps I saw a flicker of shadow. Perhaps it was just intuition. Whatever the cause, I glanced up just in time to see Michelle dumping a bucket of lake water over me.

I shouldn't have been surprised. She had told me, on the way to camp, that she was looking forward to our annual water fight. I had not told her that this year I was prepared for it. I had visited the toy store, and bought myself one of the new water guns that pumps up with air pressure and shoots a stream of water as thick as my little finger up to a 30-foot distance.

I yelped as the chilly water soaked through my T-shirt. "Water fight! Water fight!" shouted Sanjan in his fractured English. He started splashing water at the two of us. The other two youngsters at the camp, both of them granddaughters of the seniors, joined in the fun. The seniors themselves perked up and watched expectantly.

I raced off to my cabin to get the water gun. That, I realized later, was a mistake. For after I had gotten revenge on Michelle, I passed the gun to the children. Sanjan grabbed it away from the two little girls.

Seconds later, he had it perched on his hip, firing jets of water randomly into the air.

One of the girls wanted to get the gun back again. "No!" shouted Sanjan, his voice hoarse with excitement. "I got gun! I got power!"

THE IMAGE OF DEATH AND KILLING

He was only ten, and the gun itself was harmless. But his stance, the way he handled the gun, the way he discharged it into the sky, almost exactly matched a picture I had seen the week before in a national newsmagazine. Only that photo was of Monrovia, in Liberia, where a veneer of civilization and democracy had disintegrated into civil war. And the weapons that a group of teenaged boys held against their hips were machine guns – AK47s and Uzzis.

In that instant, the veil that isolates me from mindless violence, from permeating evil, was torn in two.

I had seen the same picture, I realized, most evenings on television news. The heady, infatuating power of the gun. It was the same, whether the pictures came from Afghanistan, Somalia, Gaza, Chechnya. Boys who would otherwise have been showing off climbing trees or racing bicycles showed off with high powered automatic weapons, blasting anything that moved – cat, dog, or enemy – with lethal slugs.

Sanjan had spent the first ten years of his life in that environment. For him, Rock Lake was the exception; the authority of the gun was the rule. I don't think he was evil. I think he simply assumed a role he had seen acted out almost every day of his life until he came to Canada.

But for the rest of us, it was a shock. Television, though it showed us these scenes of senseless violence, also distanced us from them. These things happened somewhere else. Suddenly, they were happening among us.

The warm afternoon took on a distinct chill, quite different from the coldness of the water still soaking our shirts. I took the gun away from Sanjan, over his protests.

LIVING IN A BUBBLE OF PEACE

The bubble of peace that I like to think I inhabit is very fragile. Most of the people I meet are honest and more or less trustworthy. If I can't trust them, it's more from their lack of competence than from any malice or malevolence on their part.

I've been fortunate all my life. I did not have abusive parents, nor was I mistreated by my teachers or other authority figures. I have not had to live with an alcoholic or a drug addict. And while my family has experienced four deaths through terminal illness, including our 21-year-old son, we have never felt victimized by their suffering, or ours. Life has been very good to me, to us.

Yet almost daily, I'm reminded of how little separates my world from a much more bitter, violent, and evil world.

A phone call comes from a woman in Toronto. She's dying. In her youth, she believes, she was experimented on by a small cult of Satan worshippers. In her prime, she had the kind of mind that could vanquish most men's egos with half her brain tied behind her back. Now turning 50, blind, bedridden, she still finds herself burning periodically with bursts of irrational rage.

Another acquaintance spent three years documenting her mother's maltreatment of her. "My mother," she explains, almost emotionlessly, "was not a very nice woman." Her memories of abuse did not surface until both her parents had died. Lacking any means of checking the accuracy of her memories, she wondered for a while if she were going crazy. Then, unexpectedly, she received corroboration of an almost uncheckable detail. She remembered stopping, with her mother, at a train station, a flag stop. The maps said there was no such place. The railway timetables said there was no such stop. But an elderly engineer, by a chance contact, confirmed that there had once been an asylum, run by a group of nuns, at such a place, where the train stopped only by pre-arrangement.

"Now I know why my shoulder dislocates so easily," she continued. "That was how she punished me. She twisted my arm until my shoulder popped out. I spent whole nights banging my back against my bedroom wall, trying to get it back in. That went on until I was 18 and big enough to defend myself physically."

A writer described following a truck along a country road, late one night. The red taillights of the truck, the pool of light from its headlights, the gravel shoulders racing by, lulled him into a kind of hypnosis. Suddenly, two small eyes glowed pink far ahead. The headlights picked up the fur of a raccoon, well over to the other side of the road. The truck swerved right across the road to smash the defenseless animal, and then swerved back again. It was clearly a deliberate and callous act of cruelty. The truck roared on into the night, while my acquaintance stopped to put the broken body out of its agony.

I live in a wonderful rural community, small enough that almost everyone can know everyone else. There's hardly such a thing as a stranger. Adults and young people interact daily. Yet not even we are protected from evil.

It was here, about two years ago, that Rodney Bell narrowly escaped a car accident when a carload of teenagers drove through a stop sign. Bell followed them, within the speed limits, to a local shopping center. He got out of his car to talk with them about responsible driving.

That evening, a group of teenagers came to Rod Bell's house. They yelled abuse at him. One of them – whose identity is protected because he was under age – hit Bell on the head with an axe. Bell will never recover fully from the attack.

A SHOCK OF REALIZATION

The veil that shields people like me from evil is indeed very fragile. It rips unexpectedly, with the same kind of shock as falling through thin ice into frigid water. Suddenly, our sheltered existence dissolves. We find ourselves floundering in a world where the comfortable conventions don't apply.

We are all, I think, uncomfortably aware of the presence of evil, closer at hand than we would like. We recognize it when an orderly picket line erupts into violence, when a young child is raped and murdered. Or when a burglar beats an elderly woman to death with a baseball bat just because she happened to be home when he broke in. Or when we hear about a Paul Bernardo, who raped a number of women in Scarborough, and then, with the help of Karla Homolka, abducted, raped, and murdered two more. (And who, if that wasn't enough, brazenly videotaped his own offenses so that he could "enjoy" them again, later.) We find ourselves locking our doors, even if we're going no further than the back garden. We install security systems and motion-detecting lighting. We wonder if we can trust our seatmates on a plane or bus.

Statistics tell us that the incidence of violent crime has actually been decreasing in Canada, but still we live in more fear than we used to. And we respond to that fear by demanding more punitive retaliation against offenders. California, always out in front on these matters, has pushed this attitude to an extreme. They've enacted a "three strikes and you're out" law: three criminal convictions and you receive an automatic life sentence. No exceptions. The radio announced one morning that police arrested more than 900 people for passively attempting to prevent logging equipment from cutting into a stand of old-growth redwood trees. Some of those people might – now or later – be sentenced to life imprisonment, ironically enough, for attempting to protect life.

This fear of omnipresent evil manifests itself in a variety of other ways. Women won't walk home at night; they call a taxi. Schools order teachers and counselors not to touch students, for any reason. Elderly citizens cross the road to avoid knots of noisy teens. Gas stations require payment before you fill up. In all probability, nothing at all has changed from when those same women walked home from the bus, teachers occasionally gave hugs to depressed students, and people paid for their gas after getting it. One day, one evening, these things were all considered safe; the next, they were too risky to continue. Nothing had changed but the perception, but that was enough.

That's how fear of evil affects us. It seeps insidiously into our thoughts and our feelings, and changes the way we react to situations.

2

MAKING EVIL POSSIBLE

Evil doesn't just happen. It starts with an attitude.

The mindset that makes evil possible has traditionally been called "sin."

The mindset matters. Evil is, in a sense, our recognition that things have gone wrong. Damage is being done. Something or someone is being hurt. But these bad things don't always result from bad motivations.

The radio news carried a report from Grozny, capital of the breakaway Russian region of Chechnya. The Chechnyan rebels and the Russian armed forces had just agreed to a cease fire. Displaced families were returning to their devastated homes. The interviewer talked to a father. The day before, the father had been shooting at Russian soldiers. He was glad to set aside his weapons, he said, through a translator. He was sick of all the killing. He hadn't wanted to go to war, but he felt he had no choice – it was either fight or yield to what he thought of as foreign forces.

His eight-year-old son, on the other hand, was sorry the fighting had ended. He looked forward, he said, to growing up so that he could have a machine gun and kill Russian soldiers too.

That boy is probably too young to understand the meaning of "sin." But he illustrated it perfectly. I could not presume, at this comfortable distance, to label the father's motivation in fighting for independence as a sin. But I can safely argue that a desire to kill for the excitement of killing is sinful. The motives of father and son differed diametrically.

ENDS AND MEANS

Some will, I'm sure, insist that killing is killing. Motivation doesn't matter – only the result counts. I hesitate to offer excuses for war. Personally, I consider violence of any kind – with wholesale war the ultimate example – to be an admission of failure to achieve results by more civilized and humane means. But it seems to me that something more needs to be considered than purely the outcome. The end neither justifies nor renders irrelevant the means.

When Robert Latimer left his seriously handicapped daughter inside his truck, running inside a closed garage, he asphyxiated her. As far as we know, death by carbon monoxide poisoning is painless. The court ruled that it was premeditated murder. For that, the judge imposed a mandatory minimum ten-year prison sentence.

Legally, Latimer's crime was exactly parallel to the crime of a hired assassin who relentlessly stalks and shoots his prey, perhaps leaving the victim to die in a spreading pool of blood. Both murders involve a single individual. Both murders are planned.

But are they really identical? Latimer may well have been mistaken about the hopelessness of his daughter's condition, as a number of organizations devoted to the rights of handicapped persons have argued. (And again, I must stress, I do not condone disposing of some other person who has become an inconvenience.) But there was ample evidence that Latimer had been a loving father. He and his wife had given their daughter selfless care for many years. Although I cannot approve of his action, I have to argue that his motivation for ending his daughter's life differs vastly from the motives of an assassin, a terrorist, a serial killer.

The law cannot make such distinctions. It can only judge the action. Traditionally, it has fallen to religion to examine motivations. And religion has described those motivations as sin.

SIN FALLS OUT OF FAVOR

Sin is not a concept our society is comfortable talking about.

Once upon a time, not that long ago, couples who chose to live together without the sanction granted by an ordained minister through a wedding ceremony were said to be "living in sin." Less politely, they were "shacking up." I haven't heard the phrase "living in sin" for over a decade. Even the concept seems meaningless when Canadian law has decreed that unmarried persons living together for a specified period shall be treated as if they were legally married. If they separate, their property and wealth is split between them, just as if they were married.

In fact, very few things that once carried the stigma of "sin" are prohibited anymore, legally or socially. Several of my friends are gay or lesbian couples. They're probably truer to each other than most heterosexual couples – certainly if television does, as it claims, merely reflect society as a whole. Yet not that long ago, those couples would have been burned at the stake for their "sin." Did you ever wonder where the derisive term "faggots" came from? A faggot is a bundle of sticks or twigs bound together for burning. They were kindling, piled around the feet of the victim. To call someone a "faggot" implied a threat that went a lot further than personal disapproval of an alternate lifestyle.

We even hesitate to use the word "sinful" to describe behavior we deplore. Personally, I'm appalled when I see a hillside clear-cut, stripped of all its trees, naked and shivering. I'm offended by mine tailings, piles of uneconomic ore abandoned to seep metallic toxins into a trout stream. And I am infuriated by economic policies that place profits at any price ahead of human misery. But, despite my disapproval, even my disgust, I usually stop short of charging the perpetrators of these actions with sin.

Sin has not disappeared. We just don't talk about it anymore. Well, at least, not as "sin." Sin is a term that belongs to bygone eras of inquisitions and witch hunts. It has connotations of an authoritarian church that kept its people in line through fear and ignorance.

We have pretty much banished sin to history books and the rarefied air of theology lectures. It's no longer part of our daily vocabulary. Even the Roman Catholic Church, which clings to tradition in so many other ways, has largely dispensed with the private confession of personal sins in favor of generalized confessions by the whole community.

We certainly don't like to talk about our own behavior as sin – though, in my experience, most people still love to gloat over other people's sins and a host of national tabloids would go broke if we didn't. Of course, the tabloids themselves rarely label the social extravagances they report on as sin.

DENYING THE REALITY OF SIN

Today, we deal with sin in one of two ways. We're more likely to celebrate it, perhaps with smirks and giggles – nudge nudge, wink wink – than to censure it. And we're more likely to rationalize and justify it – to find some kind of argument to prove that we were actually right to do whatever we did – than to repent of it.

Two situations come to mind, both of which I know about only secondhand. By coincidence, both involve what the Ten Commandments called adultery, extramarital sexual relations.

In one, a man had an affair, over several years, with the wife of his best friend from high school days. Eventually, the undercover liaison became public. The woman left her husband to live with her lover. Her husband committed suicide.

In another, a couple separated, somewhat acrimoniously. Within a week, the husband's brother moved in with the wife.

In both cases, the adulterous parties had guilt feelings. But rather than seek some way to make amends, the traditional response to sin, both preferred to defend their behavior as natural, inevitable, and necessary. They had no choice. They were in love. And love, as our society continually proclaims, is the ultimate virtue. Therefore they must have done right, not wrong.

Big corporations, of course, do exactly the same thing to justify logging an old-growth forest, downsizing their employees onto the sidewalks, or manipulating national currencies on international money markets for private gain. Economic realities give them no choice – therefore they must have done right.

Some, hearing this bad news, will simply lament the decline in traditional morality. They'll blame these social and personal ills on a breakdown of Christian values. If only people would obey the Ten Commandments, they'll say.

I don't accept that premise. It's a simplistic solution that ignores the racism of the Crusades, the oppression of slavery, the bigotry of witch hunts. By defining Arabs, slaves, or women as slightly less than fully human, not quite made "in the image of God," the dominant religious powers of those times were able to reinterpret with impunity the traditional commandments against killing, adultery, and looting.

ACTIONS AND MINDSETS

As any number of scholars have noted, the Ten Commandments fall into two groups. The first four all deal, in one way or another, with our relationship with God. The next six all relate, one way or another, to how we deal with each other: don't lie, don't steal, don't kill, keep your sex within marriage, respect your elders, and don't covet what others have. Notice – all but one of those are visible actions. Only one is an attitude. In the relatively confined tribal society in which those commandments were defined – and they were, in fact, a distillation of some 600 other, much more specific rules and regulations that are also in those early books of the Bible – it was fairly easy to identify murder, theft, adultery, and perjury.

But coveting is an attitude. Unless you happen to talk about it, it would be hard for someone else to know that you went green with envy over your neighbor's prize camel or Mercedes. Unless you fondled a neighbor's son or daughter at the campfire or the water cooler, how would anyone know you lusted after them?

That's why, by the time the Seven Deadly Sins got defined, they were entirely attitudes. Emotions. Character traits: pride, anger, envy or jealousy, lust, gluttony (including drunkenness), covetousness or greed, and sloth or laziness. Because the list-makers who defined those Seven Deadly Sins recognized something significant. "The evil that men do" – to quote Shakespeare – results from their mindset.

The Greek word that we usually translate as "evil" was *kakia,* church historian and theologian Elaine Pagels wrote in her bestselling book, *The Gnostic Gospels.* It literally meant "what is bad" and both the Greeks and the early Christians applied it to whatever one would "want to avoid, such as physical pain, sickness, suffering, misfortune, every kind of harm."

The orthodox interpreted evil (*kakia*) primarily in terms of violence against others (this giving the moral connotation of the term). They revised the Mosaic Code, which prohibits physical violation of others – murder, stealing, adultery – in terms of Jesus' prohibition of even mental and emotional violence – anger, lust, hatred.

That is, the Ten Commandments, from about 1800 BCE, say, "You must not kill." The Christians of the first century took the command further; they said, "You must not allow the emotion that leads to killing – anger."

It was a reasonable extrapolation. After all, it was Jesus who told his disciples, "Everyone who looks at a woman with lust has already committed adultery with her in his heart" (Matthew 5:28, NRSV). Lust was the emotion that made possible the prohibited action: "You shall not commit adultery."

The evil we perceive all around us is made evident in actions. Those actions happen only because certain people think in certain ways. Robertson Davies put that thought this way, in his novel *The Rebel Angels*: "Evil isn't what one *does*, it's something one *is* that infects everything one does" (emphasis added).

The sin is the mindset.

That's a definition worth keeping in mind, as we push on into this book.

3
ORIGINS OF THE SEVEN DEADLY SINS

List makers helped people sort out what's important from what's trivial.

Unfortunately, there's no agreement on what constitutes a sin. There never has been. Every culture has developed its own list of sins. As humans, we seem to have an innate compulsion to organize and categorize things. Some psychologists now argue that this – rather than tool making, or having an opposable thumb and forefinger – may be the unique characteristic of the human species.

From the beginning, for example, young babies try to make sense of things. They have no genetic programming that teaches them a specific language. Identical twins, brought up in two different cultures, will learn totally different languages, that may have radically different structures and vocabularies. But whether that language is English or Hungarian or Swahili, they will learn it at about the same stage of their development. In fact, they can learn two or more languages at the same time, with equal fluency.

I did. My parents were missionaries in India. I grew up learning both Hindi and English simultaneously. I switched back and forth from one to the other without effort, often in mid-sentence. Yet somehow I recognized that these were separate languages. My earliest recollection of language is of realizing that I was daydreaming, in a language – and that language was Hindi, not English.

CREATING ORDER OUT OF CHAOS

We learn a language and a culture. But we can only do that because we are apparently genetically programmed to categorize sights and sounds and experiences. Like God, in the biblical story of creation, we attempt to create order out of chaos. Life is, at first, pure chaos. Nothing makes sense. But an infant's initial development comes stunningly fast. Newborn babies quickly learn to differentiate mommy-types from daddy-types. Then mommy from other women, and daddy from other men. They identify colors, and shapes, and so on. Even at six months, a child psychologist told me, children will group objects according to an evident pattern: perhaps color, perhaps shape, perhaps feel. Their sorting reveals that they are making order out of chaos. Similarly, as infants, we begin to sort sounds into meaningful patterns. We try out these tentative patterns, and feed back our mistakes and successes to refine our understanding of the language.

In the same way, we attempt to name and to categorize the experiences that cause us pain, so that we can avoid them in future. (We also categorize the experiences that cause pleasure, so that we can repeat them, but that's a different subject.)

The painful experiences that have harmful social consequences we have traditionally called sins. That's a significant distinction. If, as a small child exploring Mommy's kitchen, I reach out and touch a hot stove, I will hurt myself. But there are not likely to be any further social consequences. If, as a child, I knock over and smash my mother's prized heirloom vase, I probably will not hurt myself at all. But I will be hurt, nevertheless: perhaps from a scolding, perhaps from a spanking, perhaps from being banished to my room. The second experience has social consequences, the first does not.

No culture that I have heard of considers it a sin to break your toe by stumbling over a rock. Nor is it a sin to fall out of a tree, or to have a car accident. Unless, of course, your parents specifically told you to stay out of that tree, or the car accident results from carelessness or harms an innocent bystander. Then they turn into disobedience, or criminal negligence.

Words like "disobedience" or "negligence" are the way we categorize those harmful and damaging actions. And there are literally thousands of them.

To simplify matters, every culture – and perhaps every person – attempts to organize these "sins" into some kind of order of importance. Every culture will come up with a different list. Some of those lists overlap, just as the ideals of different religions often overlap – leading some to assume that a kind of universal religion can be evoked from these similarities.

ORIGINS OF THE SEVEN DEADLY SINS

The so-called Seven Deadly Sins are one of those many lists. The number seven is an accident, sort of. Seven was a magical number in most of the ancient world. That's why there were Seven Wonders of the World, Seven Pillars of Wisdom, and so on.

So it was natural, when theologians started setting up lists of the worst things you could do, they settled on the Seven Deadly Sins. But there was no suggestion that seven was a limit. Rather, these seven were a distillation of the major sins, the ones that caused the most trouble for human society.

To counterbalance the sins, there was also a comparable list of virtues. Also seven: faith, hope, charity or love, prudence, justice, fortitude or courage or perseverance, and temperance or moderation. The first three came specifically from St. Paul's letter to the Corinthians which summarized the Christian virtues: "And now faith, hope, and love abide… and the greatest of these is love" (1 Corinthians 13:13, NRSV). The other four came from Greek philosophers, and were simply taken into the Christian tradition as a convenient summary of human ethics.

Actually, the first distillations reduced rather unwieldy lists of sins to eight, not seven. According to Professor Henry Chadwick of Cambridge, a Greek Christian named Evagrius, living out in the Egyptian desert, whittled some of the existing lists of sins down to eight. Making up lists of vices was a kind of parlor game in those days. As Professor Chadwick commented on the CBC program *Ideas:* "It was a hobby for moralists, and we have in fact one pre-Christian text which, believe it not, produces in succession 144 vices in a great row. It makes you feel there was a lot to be said for reducing the number to eight."

Evagrius' list corresponded fairly closely to ours – indicating, perhaps, that sinning hasn't changed all that much over the centuries. He included anger, gluttony, envy, covetousness, sloth, and lust. His main difference was that he split pride into two variants: boasting, and playing God.

About 100 years later, some 1400 years ago, Pope Gregory the Great decided both those forms of pride could be combined, and thus brought the list down to seven. We can only speculate about Pope Gregory's reasons for wanting the sins to number seven. But, as I've suggested, I suspect the change had something to do with symbolism. The concluding book of the New Testament, the Revelation of St. John, put a lot of emphasis on the symbolism of numbers. John of Patmos, the author of Revelation, chose 666 as "the mark of the beast" – it was one short on all counts of the magic number 777. But then he had to go beyond human perfection to find a number for God, so he picked 888.

If eight pertains to God, it hardly seems appropriate for a list of sins. After all, sins stood in opposition to God's will.

The order of the sins on the list fluctuated for a while. Pope Gregory put pride first, and lust last. That's because he saw lust as merely a sin of the flesh, while pride was a sin of the spirit. Like Lucifer, the fallen angel, pride aims too high. It attempts to usurp the position of God.

But eventually the list settled down. Thomas Aquinas, one of the Roman Catholic Church's all-star thinkers, provided the classic treatment of it in his *Summa Theologiae.* These particular sins were "deadly," he argued, not because they were necessarily worse or more heinous, but because each sin "gives rise to others, especially in the manner of final cause." That is, these are the root sins, the ones that underlie all others:

1. vainglory or pride
2. covetousness
3. lust
4. envy
5. gluttony, which included drunkenness
6. anger
7. and sloth.

These terms are not carved in stone. Other words have been used. The late Robertson Davies, in his book *The Cunning Man*, created an acronym for them: VELAWIG. The initials stood for Vanity, Envy, Lechery, Avarice, Wrath, Idleness, and Gluttony.

COMPARING LISTS

Other cultures also have their own lists of sins. And it is sometimes informative to compare them. Steve Roney, a friend currently teaching English at a university in Korea, sent me a list of the deadly sins of Korean Buddhism. There are, according to him, ten:

1. killing
2. sexual immorality
3. falsehood
4. deceit
5. theft
6. covetousness
7. adultery
8. foolishness
9. anger
10. stealing.

There are some obvious similarities between the two lists. Anger and covetousness appear on both Christian and Buddhist lists. So does sexual transgression. Killing and falsehood are not on the Christian list of deadly sins, but are clearly paralleled in the Ten Commandments.

The most obvious difference, though, is the inclusion of one item – foolishness. "The Western tradition is the reverse," Steve noted. "We think there is moral superiority in innocence. Hence the heroism of Forrest Gump."

In the Western world, Steve suggests, "figures of evil are often the learned or the intelligent, feeding a tradition of anti-intellectualism. Faust. Frankenstein. Moriarty... The idea goes back to the Garden of Eden. The first family was tempted by the clever snake ('the most subtle of beasts') to eat of knowledge (of the tree of the knowledge of good and evil)."

Adam and Eve, he continues, "wanted 'to become as gods, knowing good and evil.' The original sin was not sex; the original sin looks more like knowledge!"

All religions have something like a Garden of Eden myth, a time of original innocence, a time of lack of knowledge. Buddhism had one too. For Buddhists, it happened in the life of Siddhartha Gautama. Until he was 29 years old, the man who would be the first Buddha lived in a kind of Eden, protected, within the walls of his father's palace, from harsh reality. Finally, one day, he persuaded a trusted servant to take him outside. There, for the first time, he encountered sickness, death, and poverty. The shock of knowledge sent him on a seven-year search for enlightenment – which became, in time, Buddhism.

For both traditions, then, Eden was literally "a fool's paradise." The difference between Buddhism and the Jewish, Christian, and Islamic traditions is that Buddhists declared ignorance to be the sin; Christians, Jews, and Muslims preferred to honor the time of innocence.

Although he himself is a devout Roman Catholic, Steve Roney says: "I support the Eastern view. In practice, we must take stupidity to be culpable. Sure, you can argue that one is not responsible for how intelligent one is. But it is just as easy to argue that one is not responsible for one's temperament."

A CLIMATE OF ANTI-INTELLECTUALISM

It makes a lot of sense. In fact, by indicating that things *ought* to make sense, I imply that intelligence is valuable. And most people would agree. Yet it seems to me that Steve Roney is onto something here. We *do* have a deep suspicion of intelligence in the Western world. Innocence equates with naïvity. Would Shirley Temple still be as adorable with Albert Einstein's mind? Or with Mother Teresa's experience in the squalid slums of Calcutta? Would anyone watch the Simpsons if they were all members of Mensa?

Americans distrust intelligence. In the United States, the electorate rejected acknowledged intellectuals Adlai Stevenson II and George McGovern in favor of Dwight Eisenhower and Richard Nixon, respectively. No one is likely to accuse Ronald Reagan or George Bush of being intellectual heavyweights. There have been some brilliant politicians: John Kennedy comes to mind, along with his brother Robert. Or, in an earlier time, Abraham Lincoln. Significantly, all three were assassinated.

Europeans may place a higher value on intelligence – I don't know enough about their society to comment. But I suspect a similar bias there, too. And despite Steve Roney's optimism about Eastern thought, I'm inclined to think that there's a kind of *universal* paranoia against those who may be more intelligent than ourselves. In Russia, Stalin systematically purged his nation's intelligentsia to the Gulag work camps. In China, the professors and teachers were the prime target of Mao's Red Guards. In Cambodia, the intellectual elite were the first dispatched from the cities to the killing fields.

Strange, isn't it? The one quality that we humans consistently claim distinguishes us from the animals becomes a quality that we distrust.

But it's typical of the way our values and vices get mixed up. Sometimes it's difficult to know which is which.

4

Trivializing Sin

The ways we invent to evade dealing with the troublesome questions of sin.

When I started writing this book, I wanted to call it, "Whatever Became of Sin?" Unfortunately, someone else had taken that title already: Karl Menninger, the founder of the Menninger Clinics. He wrote *Whatever Became of Sin?* back in 1973.

His title wasn't suggesting that we didn't sin anymore. Rather, he argued, we had found some new ways of describing sin that didn't make it *sound* like sin anymore.

Here are three of the ways that Menninger thought we avoid dealing with the reality of sin.

1. SIN AS ILLNESS

We treat sin as an illness. It may be psychological, or physical, or chemical. Whatever the cause, the illness controls the behavior, not the person. Therefore the illness is to blame, not the person.

There's a nice touch to that theory. In a labor dispute I got involved in, not by choice, the management consultant told us, "Concentrate on the problem, not on the person." It's a modern variant of the old adage,

"Condemn the sin, not the sinner." His advice taught us not to blame all of the company's problems on one particular member, as if that one personality had somehow caused everyone else's failings.

Treating sin as illness also offers hope. Illnesses are curable – or at least treatable. Even terminal illnesses like cancer or cystic fibrosis can have their effects eased. As a result, there is not as much social stigma attached to an illness as to a sin. (AIDS still has a stigma attached to it, as leprosy did in ancient times. But as we learn more about AIDS, and realize how many people contracted it through no fault of their own – through blood transfusions, for example, or within the bounds of faithful marital sex – even that stigma is fading.)

But blaming the illness still removes responsibility from the person who harmed others.

2. TRANSFORM IT INTO CRIME

Second, we make sin a crime. This shifts the responsibility from the moral to the legal sphere. "What had been the business of priests," Menninger wrote, "becomes the business of the police, assisted by lawyers and judges and jailers. Between them, they seek and seize, detain, hold, humble, hurt, deport, execute, or discharge their 'sinners,' now called criminals."

This shift is not, in itself, a bad thing. If I were accused of a crime – rightly or wrongly – I would certainly rather trust even a corrupt justice system than an angry mob. I first went to Haiti while the infamous "Papa Doc" Duvalier governed with the support of his thugs, the "Tonton Macoutes." I worried about lawlessness. I constantly checked my wallet, my passport, my camera. "Don't worry about theft," my host reassured me. "If you accused someone of stealing something from you, the local people would descend on him before he got a block away and beat him up so badly he'd be grateful if the police arrived in time to take over the job."

But this transformation of sin also has a negative effect. It removes responsibility from us. We no longer need to strive for harmonious relationships in our neighborhood; we call the police. We no longer need to support abused families; we call in the social workers. Like Pontius Pilate, we have found a way to wash our hands of the evil going on around us.

It also grants us a way to deny that any wrongdoing has happened. If it was legal, it couldn't be wrong. I hear this argument so often, I'm amazed that those who make it don't realize the underlying assumption they make. A company dumps toxic wastes in a river or a landfill site. Even though later experience shows conclusively that those wastes poisoned a whole town's wells, or irreparably damaged children's nervous systems, the companies disavow responsibility. They acted within government guidelines, they insist. So it must have been right.

On the news, today, I heard that a logging company with a history of environmental infractions had clear-cut a river delta supposedly preserved for studies of grizzly bear habitat. The forest has been savaged. It will never revert to its previous state. The company insists it did nothing wrong. It received a permit from local officials who, apparently, had not known of the protection provisions. Therefore, the company considers itself absolved.

Futurist Reuben "Butch" Nelson identified the fallacy of this argument years ago. In an interview, he told me: "Businesses claim they are being good corporate citizens because they do only what the law allows. But would you call someone a good husband if he did for his wife only the minimum required by law? Would you call someone a good member of the community if she did no more than municipal regulations required of her? Of course not!"

3. BLAMING SOCIETY

Third, we treat sin as collective irresponsibility, the inevitable product of a dysfunctional society. The group or the "system" is responsible, not the individual. People don't commit crimes because they are bad, but because they were abused as children, or were brought up in the wrong neighborhood, or were adversely affected when their mothers indulged in drugs or smoking or alcohol during pregnancy. They don't sin; they are innocent victims of circumstances beyond their control.

The notion of collective responsibility, particularly, removes any blame from the person or the individual. As comedian Anna Russell cracked, in one of her skits, "Everything I do that's wrong is someone else's fault!"

But there's an implicit assumption involved here, that sins are only done by individuals. If it can't be blamed on a single individual, then it can't have been wrong. Period.

As an example, consider the Atlantic cod fishery. There were thousands of people involved in overfishing cod stocks that had been called "inexhaustible" for 500 years. But no one person could be held responsible for the debacle. It wasn't my fault, everyone would say. If I stopped fishing, I would hurt only myself. Everyone else was doing it.

Someone might argue that the ultimate responsibility rested with the federal minister of fisheries, who permitted the slaughter to continue too long. But he could counter that he was simply acting on information given to him. By others. By a whole culture of fisheries experts and researchers. He was protecting people's livelihood. So it couldn't be his fault. And besides, he was just carrying out the mandate given to him by his constituents. If anyone's to blame, they must be.

If no one person did wrong, goes the assumption, then whatever it was can't have been wrong. By this assumption, a sin – to be a sin at all – must be traceable to a single individual.

LIMIT IT TO THE PERSONAL REALM

Karl Menninger didn't explore this notion, but that's yet another way that we avoid dealing with sin. We limit it to the personal level. We privatize it. We trivialize sin by treating it exclusively as a personal matter.

This obsession with pinning the blame onto an individual – or, lacking such an individual, onto a single organization – surfaced over and over again during the Krever Commission's inquiry into Canada's tainted blood supplies. During the early 1980s, more than 1,000 people received blood products tainted with HIV and hepatitis, either as transfusions or as treatment for hemophilia. Many of those infected have since died of AIDS or other diseases. So far, only the Canadian Hemophilia Society has had the integrity to admit that it could have done more to protect hemophiliacs. The Red Cross, which operated the blood supply system, and the government, which set up the rules under which the Red Cross operated, both went to court to try to prevent Justice Horace Krever from blaming *anyone* for doing wrong.

Both Krever and the litigants assumed that if something bad had happened, someone must have done it. It's simply taken for granted that there must be a person behind the harm done.

It follows, therefore, that if no one can be blamed, nothing wrong happened.

Yet it is entirely possible that in such a situation, an enormous wrong was done, but no one person was responsible.

COMMUNITY CONSCIOUSNESS

Earlier this century, psychoanalyst Carl Jung identified what he called the collective unconscious. Collectively, we are more than just the sum of our personal experiences. I heard someone protest, on an open line show, that "all this talk about community benefits is bullshit, because a community is nothing more than the individuals who comprise it." I can only assume that man was not married. Because a marriage is always either more or less than two separate individuals. Nor, I presume, has he ever played for a sports team; any team transcends or restrains the capabilities of its individual players. Any collective group is always more – or less – than the sum of its parts.

On an even larger scale, none of us are just isolated individuals. We are products of our histories, our myths, our social assumptions. As a psychoanalyst, Jung worked with individual clients, so he saw this collective unconscious shaping the reactions of a single person. But the concept applies equally well to groups. Every group is shaped both by its origins and its personnel. The General Assembly of The Presbyterian Church in Canada will do things "decently and in good order," regardless of the membership of that particular assembly, because that's the way Presbyterians do things. A group of Hell's Angels motorcyclists, by contrast, will have their own very different understanding of order, let alone of decency.

Yet both are more than simply an amalgam of the participants. A mob is not simply a mindless body manipulated by an evil leader. Palestinians are not simply pawns pushed around by Yasser Arafat, nor have Iraqis sold their souls to Saddam Hussein – however much the North American mass media may try to portray them that way. But neither is a mob a rational consensus among all its members. It develops a mind of its own, often ignoring the pleas of its leaders for peace, for cease-fire. Indeed, a mob may behave in ways that not one of its members would later endorse.

By even mentioning a mob, I'm probably prejudicing my case. Because even good-hearted individuals can get mired in collective sin.

Think about young Tiger Woods, for example. He's a 20-year-old golf pro, widely regarded as the next superstar. In his first season as a pro, after winning the US Amateur title the year before, he ranked high in winnings. He is, by all reports, an immensely likable young man. During the Canadian Open, his gallery of fans grew bigger with every hole he played. Hardly anyone, it seemed, had a bad word to say about him. Not even his competitors.

But no matter how good Tiger Woods is, no matter how well he gets along with other golf pros and sports fans, I'm told that there are still 12 golf courses in the US where he cannot play. Because he's black.

PERSONAL MORALITY MISSES THE POINT

Is that the fault of one bigoted person at each of those courses? Has any one group or organization conspired to keep Woods out? Hardly likely. They're trapped by a mentality they don't even recognize.

As a young journalist, I was sent to South Africa to cover the trial of Geoffrey ffrench-Beytagh. He was the dean of the Anglican Cathedral in Johannesburg. He was accused of aiding terrorism because he opposed apartheid.

My first exposure to apartheid came as I stepped out of the Johannesburg airport. Johannesburg can be cool in the evenings. A shiny new pickup truck whirled by. A white man wearing a bulky hand-knitted turtleneck sweater sat behind closed windows inside the heated cab. A black man wearing a shirt and pants that looked as if they had been put through a shredder huddled in the back, shivering in the chill air.

Later, I walked the streets of Johannesburg, and of Pretoria, the capital of South Africa. A sense of anger hung over the sidewalks, as a few privileged whites rode on slick air-conditioned buses, while blacks lined up to pack themselves into rickety vehicles that didn't even run on the same streets. I watched blacks cleaning up playgrounds in which their children could never play.

And I remember thinking, If violence breaks out here, no one is going to care if I support black aspirations. No one will care how good my personal relationships are with oppressed minorities, here or back home. They will simply see me as white, and start shooting.

Personal morality did not offer me – or any other liberally minded whites – immunity against the taint of apartheid, the collective sin of South African society. It doesn't absolve anyone, anywhere, of collective sins.

UNWILLING TO SHARE GUILT

I find it interesting that no one uses Menninger's "collective" explanation for sins that are genuinely collective. Even when it can be definitively shown that our North American economic policies have made life worse, not better, for people in developing countries, you don't hear anyone saying, "Yes, we're responsible."

The people in our valley remain collectively addicted to burning off their leaves in the autumn. In the spring, they burn off the long grass from last summer. Air quality up and down the valley plummets. People with respiratory problems – asthma, emphysema, bronchitis – have to stay indoors. Some have to rely on oxygen. No one says, "We're doing something wrong here. We need to change." Change, if it comes, will end up being legislated; it will not happen by consensus.

If it's everybody's fault, it's nobody's fault. And if it's nobody's fault, it's not considered a fault at all.

But if that were true, if the only sins we had to worry about were personal, there wouldn't be 27 million refugees fleeing from more than 40 civil wars around the world. If sin only happened at the personal level, there would have been no Tienanmen Square massacre in China, no disastrous megaprojects like the Narmada Dam in India, no technological catastrophes like the Chernobyl nuclear generating station in the Ukraine. The Amazon rain forest would not be slashed and burned to make room for ranch land on which to grow beef for North American hamburgers. We would simply have to deal with personal weaknesses – a bit of bragging, some jealousy, some theft, some obesity and drunkenness.

Obviously, the things that cause widespread harm are not limited to personal weaknesses. But as long as we trivialize sin by making it purely personal, we don't have to face up to the real injustices that plague our world.

MUDDYING THE WATERS

There are, in addition, two more ways we deny the reality of sin and evil. We confuse the issue. And we relativize it.

We confuse the issue by playing with words. Most of us, for example, have no difficulty distinguishing between good and bad, when given clear choices. We'll choose gentle over violent, kind over callous, sensitive over insensitive. But sin is never that easy. Suppose you also suggest that "gentle" equates with "weak," and the alternative to weak is "strong." Or "decisive." Or "effective leadership." In that case, many people will have a decided preference for strong over weak. If they approve of "effective leadership," they may well accept "harsh" or even brutal as an unfortunate but possibly unavoidable by-product.

Those who promote the idolatries of our time – economic competition, profit, exploitation of resources – are very skilled at using words that manipulate these choices. The technique is simple. You simply associate the less desirable quality with some other quality that is more desirable. People will tolerate one for the sake of the other. That is how mass layoffs that shatter loyalty built up over generations, betray trust, destroy people's self-respect, and leave thousands of former employees without hope, can be portrayed as commendable. Good management. Clearheaded decision making unswayed by sloppy sentimentalism.

Using this technique, cutthroat competition becomes corporate excellence. War becomes necessary, just, or even glorious. Wealth and power determine worth – those who have neither are automatically worthless, not worth paying any attention to.

Sin is less likely to be seen as sin, if it can hide behind the skirts of something less offensive. So we change the words. Bigotry masquerades as patriotism; ruthlessness as a prerequisite for profit.

It's a wonderfully seductive technique. And I confess that I've taught it myself. In the days when I taught business-writing skills with Eric McLuhan – son of Marshall McLuhan – we called this technique "burying it."

Suppose, for instance, that irate customers complain that your company is, say, making flower pots out of substandard clay. Don't fight with them, we said. Agree with them. The clay *is* substandard. But it's Canadian clay, not imported from Sri Lanka. It employs Canadian workers. That helps to offset the job losses of the Free Trade Agreement. It supports the Canadian economy, and a thriving Canadian economy reduces the need for tax increases. You see, you're really better off because of these substandard pots.

Of course it was unethical. But we justified it under the loftier goal of teaching people how to use their language more effectively.

We succumbed, in other words, to our own argument.

LET'S AGREE TO DISAGREE

There's one final way that people today avoid facing up to their sins. I'm surprised that Karl Menninger didn't include it – or perhaps it hadn't grown enough to be noticeable at the time he wrote his book.

We relativize things. That is, we turn issues of right and wrong into personal preference. You're entitled to your views; I'm entitled to mine. It's an appealing concept – especially if you happen to be an eccentric who doesn't quite fit the conventional mold. But it has a serious flaw in it, and I don't think I can explain that flaw better than Terry Anderson, professor of Christian Ethics at Vancouver School of Theology.

In 1986, when Vancouver held a world exposition called Expo '86, Terry visited the United Nations Pavilion. He saw a film, and wrote about it later in the VST newsletter, *Perspectives*.

"I found it long on good sentiment and short on thought," he wrote. "The vision presented was of a world in which diverse peoples live together in mutual respect, justice, and harmony..."

So far, so good.

"But the film goes on to declare that the main barrier to achieving such a world is that people make moral judgments about right and wrong, good and bad, thereby dividing the world into 'them' and 'us,' generating conflict and war."

That view might *seem* reasonable, but for an ethicist, it was like a red rag to a bull. Terry immediately identified "the inherent contradictions in such a view." As he noted, by "castigating all credos and moralities for their exclusiveness and divisiveness, this position is itself making dogmatic moral claims (you *should not* make moral judgments), dividing the world into *them* (the bad, who do such things) and *us* (the good, who subscribe to this viewpoint)."

"The real meaning of such a film," Terry went on, is "the world will be saved only if all people have *our* beliefs and values and make moral judgments by *our* standards... The troubling aspect is the illusion that a belief in inclusiveness and non-judgment is itself free from exclusive and divisive qualities."

Tolerance, in other words, quickly turns into intolerance. Relativity becomes its own absolute. Nobody's allowed to make judgments anymore. Of anything, or anybody. Regardless of what they did.

Relativism *legislates* sin out of existence.

5

Changing Standards

Old understandings of sin have evolved until
sin is almost unrecognizable today.

If Tomás de Torquemada could hear our daughter Sharon, a lifelong chocaholic, describe a double-chocolate fudge brownie dessert as "positively sinful," he would spin in his grave like a gyroscope.

Torquemada was the chief prosecutor of the Spanish Inquisition. As Grand Inquisitor, he built an unenviable reputation out of extorting confessions from his victims. He refined torture to an art unsurpassed until the superior technology of this century devised even more sophisticated ways of making victims miserable.

Edgar Allan Poe's short story, *The Pit and the Pendulum*, epitomizes for many the fiendishness of the Inquisition's efforts. Poe's imagination was better than his research. For the most part, the Inquisition was limited to techniques that induced physical pain: starving, burning, stretching on the rack, blinding, crushing joints, breaking bones.

It remained for modern times to refine torture. Year after year, Amnesty International has documented the atrocities that autocratic authorities impose on their dissident citizens. Even the crudest efforts used technology that Torquemada would have envied. Iran, in the days of the Shah, sometimes simply strapped victims to a hydraulic auto hoist, and jacked them up against the ceiling. Chile, under General Pinochet, used electric shocks on prisoners, applied both externally and internally. The Communist regime in the former Soviet Union invented psychological torture, injecting its prisoners with mind-altering drugs. Brazilian torturers added the diabolical touch of forcing their captives to watch while their wives or children were raped, tortured, or murdered.

Torquemada would have been envious. But calling a chocolate dessert sinful would have baffled him.

ROOTING OUT HERESY

The Inquisition started with good intentions. The Dominican order, which stage-managed both the Roman and the Spanish Inquisitions for the Vatican, was dedicated to seeking truth. But truth was pretty rigorously defined by the Roman Catholic Church. Then as now, the Roman church did not take kindly to dissent. It wanted to root out heresy, which it considered the most serious of sins. The church felt challenged by the new mood of what we now call "The Enlightenment," a mood which put everything up for question, which tested everything against reason and experience.

The Christian church had long before defined various levels of sin. The most serious, even unforgivable, were sins which rejected divine authority – and, by implication, the authority of God's earthly institution, the church. At the top of the list was heresy – denial of, or opposition to, an established church doctrine.

Lesser sins were divided into two groups: mortal and venial. Mortal sins were serious enough to constitute a threat to one's life – here, or in the hereafter. Murder, for example, was specifically prohibited by the Ten Commandments that God gave Moses in the desert. Even if a murderer escaped capital punishment in this life, the misdeed would preclude admission to heaven in eternal life.

Venial sins were the minor matters. They could be confessed and then countered by a prescribed act of penance. A few Hail Marys for a little white lie about Grandma's cooking, perhaps. The purchase of an "indulgence" – baldly put, a bribe to the church – for missing Mass. More serious matters – a bit of fraud in business dealings, or a romp in the hay with the local Lothario – might require a more painful, and more public, penance. Like ascending the cathedral steps on one's knees. Don't scorn such a penance. Cathedrals tended to be built on high ground, so that people always looked up to them. And climbing 100 or more stone steps on one's knees can be excruciatingly painful. I watched devout penitents doing it at the Oratory of St. Joseph, in Montreal. When I tried it myself, for just a few steps, I quickly discovered that the tears streaming down their faces did not result merely from overflowing devotion.

Mortal sins – life threatening sins – could be expiated too. But not by any single act of penance. The only hope of salvation lay in a lifetime of piety, purity, and good works. That is the central theme of writings such as *Les Miserables*. In the eyes of the law, a crime was forever a crime. But in the eyes of God, good folk could, in the end, redeem themselves.

It all sounds so dated now.

PUSHED OFF THE EDGE

People today are more likely to confess their sins to a psychiatrist or a lawyer than to a priest. And they're more likely to seek healing or acquittal than penance and redemption. In fact, I doubt if the notion of redemption even occurs to most people anymore.

Thus we have trivialized sin. We have pushed it to the edge of social consciousness. Often, it has fallen off the edge of awareness and disappeared completely.

Take blasphemy, for example.

Blasphemy was once a major sin. In the Ten Commandments, it ranks third, well ahead of murder, theft, adultery, lying, and stealing. "Thou

shalt not take the name of the Lord thy God in vain," the Commandment says.

For a long time, blasphemy was considered a sure sign of heresy. Profanity took a sacred name and made it "profane" – common, vulgar. One
would only do that if one felt contempt for the divine.

Blasphemy had to be intentional. Since hypnotism hadn't been invented yet, and there were no psychologists around to transfer the blame
onto social upbringing – Menninger's collective irresponsibility – one
could not claim that blasphemous words were uttered involuntarily. You
swore by your own choice.

And blasphemy was unforgivable. Forgiveness comes from God. But
because blasphemers in effect denied the power and authority of God,
by treating it with contempt, they had already cut themselves off from
the possibility of pardon.

Most of our expletives began as euphemisms – socially acceptable variants of what would otherwise be blasphemy. The good old American
"Gee!" is simply short for "Jesus." "Gosh!" is a way of not quite saying
"God." In old comic books, Batman's always-honorable sidekick Robin
used to utter the inoffensive epithet, "Holy Moley!" which, like "Holy
cow!" "Great Scott!" or "Heavens to Betsy," allowed the borderline excitement of pushing the limits of propriety without actually skidding over
the line into blasphemy.

If blasphemy were still considered a sin, 90 percent of North Americans would qualify for Torquemada's torture chambers.

It's hard, nowadays, to avoid hearing the Lord's name taken in vain.
Now that Joan and I no longer have children living at home, we've grown
out of touch with the language of young people. But occasionally, I walk
past a school yard and hear the children at play. Or I'm on a bus, and
find myself standing close enough to group of young people to overhear
their conversation. I am, I confess, often appalled.

Two classes of cuss-words seem to dominate. There are the ano-geni-
tal terms, of which "shit" and "fuck" are the two most basic. And there

are what Torquemada would have considered blasphemies: "God," "Jesus," and "Christ," each with a variety of supplementary additions.

If I challenged the users of these words, I'm sure that most of them would have no idea they were swearing at all.

But I shouldn't give the impression that a decline in language standards applies only to today's youth. For them, it might be little more than their natural rebellion against the standards of adult society. The change is universal.

Not that many years ago, radio and television had a self-imposed code of linguistic no-no's. One just didn't say "My God!" or "Jesus!" on air. Profanity could destroy your career. More than one announcer was fired for uttering an expletive, undeleted, by neglecting to turn off a microphone switch.

My first job was writing radio commercials. One of my clients, a local food chain, wanted to promote its cheese section. It had 42 different kinds of cheese. So, logically, I started one commercial with that information. "Cheeses!" I wrote for that client, 42 different kinds of cheeses – all yours at Woodwards Food Floors."

We had a loudspeaker in the copywriters' cramped little office, so that we could monitor the way the station's announcers mangled our precious prose. At the time scheduled for this commercial, I listened as the music ended. I heard the announcer take a breath before launching into the announcement. Over the air came a single word: "Cheeses!" Then silence. Nothing. Nothing but dead air. After what seemed like an a eternity, music returned.

The door to the copywriters' office crashed open. The announcer stormed in. Furiously, he flung a crumpled sheet of paper on my desk. "Don't you *ever* do that to me again!" he stormed.

He wasn't kidding. He thought I had tricked him into swearing on air. He was terrified he would lose his job for it.

Today, I wonder if anyone would care. In the days when I worked for the Canadian Broadcasting Corporation – that bastion of social propriety, as cautious about good taste as it was precise about pronunciation – we carefully edited out any expletives that crept into an interview. Live programs always had a built-in delay that allowed a vigilant operator to "beep" out any naughty words uttered in the heat of the moment.

Today, even staff interviewers tend to use "God" unthinkingly as an interjection. "Jesus" and "for Christ's sake" are less common, but do occur. And if that's an acceptable standard for the CBC, so sensitive to every twitch of public opinion, you can imagine what it is for the coffee shop, the assembly line, and the playground.

Profanity is simply not considered a sin anymore.

Nor is adultery, judging by the frequency with which unmarried couples leap into bed on television drama series.

STRUGGLING TO MAKE SENSE OF SIN

What's happened to our language? What's happened to our thinking?

Something has changed. Our understanding of sin has evolved, until it's almost unrecognizable. That creates problems for those of us old enough to have been brought up with a clear understanding of sin. Sin was lying or cheating or killing. Depending on our religious affiliation, sin might also be dancing, smoking, or playing cards. Today we find ourselves baffled and confused by social justice movements – of the right or of the left politically, of white, black, or native origins – that self-righteously denounce societal sins while acting in ways we used to think of as sinful. There was a time when only wild-west desperadoes and crooks blockaded roads, wore masks, and waved automatic weapons.

At the same time, those who are younger, who were brought up during a period when sin became unfashionable, find themselves floundering in a moral morass. They do sense, deep inside, that there is a difference between right and wrong. But they don't know how to define it. The old, often arbitrary, definitions no longer make sense to them.

They don't make much sense to me anymore, either. It is out of my own

struggle to make sense out of the world around me and the historic traditions I have inherited that the chapters and principles of this book evolved.

You've already encountered three of those principles: sin is an attitude, a motivation, a mindset, not just an action; sin has harmful social
consequences; and sin deals, at its roots, with beliefs.

6

Virtues and Vices

In the ethical earthquake we're living through,
it's hard to tell one from the other.

In the middle of a miserable Toronto February, with gray skies and bitter winds, I turned on the radio.

"Got the February blahs?" asked the first commercial. "Had it up to here with slush soaking your shoes, sleet stinging your ears, salt rotting your car? Are you feeling trapped by the Monday to Friday grind? Then we've got the answer for you! It's (dramatic pause for effect) SQUARE ONE!"

"Square One," in case you don't live in southern Ontario, is a shopping center. More than 300 stores. Open until nine, every night. Packed with thousands of items guaranteed to make anyone feel better.

The commercial rambled on, extolling the virtues of conspicuous consumption. The message was unmistakable: spending, like Guinness, is good for you. When you're feeling down, depressed, poor in spirit, just spend. Spending will make you feel better. It doesn't matter what you spend on, just spend.

What happened to thrift?

Once, thrift was a good thing. People saved. Spending money unnecessarily was, if not actually sinful, at least frowned upon.

But things have changed, apparently. A sale flyer from The Bay arrived with our newspaper. "The more you buy, the more you save!" screamed its headline in three-inch letters.

Spending money will not only make you feel better, it's also the new way to be thrifty! No matter that your bank account is noticeably smaller. No matter that your spending spree means there's less left for the rent payment, and the children may have to live on hamburger for the rest of the month. At least, you now have a gigantic home-movie-size TV screen on which they can watch their favorite videos. If you had bought it at regular prices, it would have wiped out your car payment too, and had the kids eating dog food. So your purchase must be thrifty. Mustn't it?

And then the other night, a television commercial showed a happy couple enthusing about how much they had "earned." They had subscribed to a new dining card. They brandished it as if they had just found the Holy Grail. When they ate at selected restaurants, they paid full price for their meals. But during the next month, they received a check in the mail. From those restaurants. For 20 percent of what they paid.

"If our restaurant bill is $100, we earn $20!" she told him happily.

"And if it's $300, we earn $60!" he responded, as if he had just had an orgasm.

A moment's thought will inform anyone that if you've got less money than you had when you started, you haven't earned anything. You haven't saved anything. And at that point, you won't feel any better either.

IN THE MIDDLE OF AN EARTHQUAKE

But that doesn't matter. Because lies are no longer unacceptable – they're the foundation of a whole industry dedicated to performing invisible surgery on your wallet.

It's an example of the confusing ways that our standards have changed. Like a sand castle swept away by the tide, the old order crumbles, and leaves us grasping for straws.

Herbert O'Driscoll, the internationally known author, preacher, and inspirational speaker, described the kind of situation we find ourselves in. He was watching television coverage of the Los Angeles earthquake, he said in an address to the annual conference of Canadian Church Press. The television crews followed a woman, a Hispanic woman, whose English was not terribly fluent, through her devastated house. She led them from the front of the house, into this darkened wreck. They followed her through the hallway, into the kitchen.

"I was standing here," she said. "The first I knew of the quake was when the dishes started to rattle in the cupboards. Then the cupboards fell off the walls. Then I tried to go out into my back yard, and the door sort of broke up as I got to it. And I went into the yard, and I could see the gravel was heaving up."

She ran to the front street, and she saw that the asphalt had split. "And that," she told the camera, "was when I knew for sure that the earth had moved." O'Driscoll drew this conclusion:

We are all living in a time of earthquake. But it is only in this decade that we can really know that the earth has moved. It started a century ago, when it was just some dishes rattling. The cupboards started to fall off the walls in the 1960s, the doors disintegrated in the 1970s, the earth started heaving in the 1980s. But it is only now, as we come toward the end of the 1990s, that we all "know for sure that the earth has moved."

Perhaps nothing symbolizes the earthquake we are living through better than the upheaval in moral values. Social commentators speak of it as a "paradigm shift." "Paradigm," as I understand it, means something much deeper than rearranging the deck chairs; it calls for a re-thinking of our basic assumptions about life that's as far-reaching as abandoning the Titanic for the lifeboats.

This shift of values has been most vigorously opposed by the religious right. They've had about as much success as King Canute ordering the tide to stop rising. It's been fascinating, over the last decade, to watch the churches that trumpeted "traditional family values," churches that ejected from membership anyone divorced or even suspected of infidelity, having to turn themselves inside out without admitting that anything had changed. "They had to," a Presbyterian minister who had just returned from an inter-denominational conference explained to me. "Or they'd have had no one left in their congregations. They simply substituted the language of pastoral care for the language of judgment and sin."

Though we may not talk much about sin anymore, that's really what we mean by euphemisms like "moral values" and "social standards." What's acceptable? What isn't?

INDISPENSABLE TO OUR SOCIETY

This has nothing to do with law. The law, typically, lags years, even generations, behind reality. Marijuana use is illegal. Yet even the president of the United States admits to having smoked it – though he insists he didn't inhale. Police forces all over the USA wage war on cocaine trafficking, yet it is apparently in common use among lawyers and law officers – not to mention doctors, professors, and show business celebrities. There's no doubt that recreational use of illegal substances used to be considered a sin. But is it still?

Our understanding of sin is part of this earthquake we are living through, part of this "paradigm shift."

Once upon a time, sins were things to be avoided. Today, what used to be called sins are often indispensable to our consumer society.

Try to imagine what would happen to the restaurant business, for example, if we outlawed gluttony.

Or to car sales, if no one coveted their neighbor's minivan or Mercedes.

Or to education – from kindergartens to universities to vocational training programs – if people had no aspirations to self-improvement, to a more affluent lifestyle.

Try to imagine what our lives would be like without all of our labor saving devices, from automatic washing machines to central heating. "Labor saving" is simply a nice way of saying "lazy." When my mother saw me staggering under an oversized load, she called it "a lazy man's burden." I thought I was working pretty hard. But the truth is, I was too lazy to make a second trip.

Every one of the historic Seven Deadly Sins has, in fact, become an essential element of some aspect of modern life in North America. That doesn't mean that our society and culture is intrinsically sinful – as tempting as that notion may be sometimes. It simply illustrates the earthquake we're currently living through.

VIRTUE AT THE CORE OF EVERY VICE

In the following chapters, I'm going to examine in more detail the roles each of these Seven Deadly Sins plays in our culture, both for good and for ill. In this chapter, however, I want to explore how it can happen that what we once called a sin has become a necessity.

Not many people really endorse pride or lust, envy or covetousness. On a personal level, these qualities are still frowned on. But in our consumer society, we simply could not do without them. They've become necessary evils.

And frankly, I would not want to do without them. If, as some Christian groups claim, the Messiah is going to return to earth one of these days and banish every sin from the face of the earth as St. Patrick is supposed to have driven the snakes out of Ireland, almost every aspect of our modern civilization would disappear. Banks would collapse, restaurants would lie empty, the clothing and cosmetic industries would go broke, movie and television screens would go blank, and good causes would fade into oblivion.

And although I rail consistently at the injustices committed by many of these modern institutions, I do not particularly want to go back to a life of grubbing on the forest floor for roots and rodents – the inevitable consequence of doing away with all the technologies spawned by the collective sloth of the human race.

I doubt if these Christian groups want that outcome either, if that is what the Second Coming of Christ means. In fact, I am convinced that conservative Christians – the kind who tend to identify themselves as "evangelicals" – are often more attached to the things of this world than they might like to admit.

Fortunately for them, and for the rest of us too, we won't have to do without all our modern conveniences. And not necessarily because their dogmas about the end of the present age are wrong – though I personally consider them misinformed, misguided, and mistaken. We won't have to, because there's no such thing as a pure sin.

That's worth repeating, because it goes against many common perceptions. Every vice has, at its core, a virtue. Every sin has a saving grace.

St. John Cassian, a disciple of Evagrius, the man who drafted that early list of eight deadly sins out in the Egyptian desert, may have been the first to recognize that truth. On the CBC program *Ideas,* Professor Henry Chadwick commented:

> Cassian was the first person to see that these (sins) are irrational and uncontrolled developments of what are in effect perfectly good primary impulses of the human heart. For example, we all experience hunger and thirst. At what point does it pass into gluttony?... He recognized that what is a perfectly good element in the constitution of the whole human nature can be distorted by a grand egotism....

THE SEVEN ESSENTIAL ELEMENTS

So let's take egotism, for example. Pride. It's simply self-esteem, a sense of personal worth, taken to an extreme.

Everyone needs some self-esteem. Without some sense of our own worth, we can't affirm the worth of anyone else. That's the origin of the term "worship." "Worship" is a shortening of an ancient English word meaning "worth-ship" – an affirming of our intrinsic worth as the subjects and family of God. Worship continues to be important for vast numbers of people. As Canadian sociologist Reginald Bibby wrote in *There's Got To Be More*, "Despite sagging attendance, the number of people attending services in a single average week (around five million in Canada) exceeds the number of fans the Blue Jays draw in an entire season – and the Jays annually lead the American League in attendance."

We need to get together in community. When we do, we commonly celebrate by feasting together. The image of the shared meal, the bounty of the earth poured forth in blessing upon this gathering, is central to our understanding of ourselves as members of families, clans, tribes, and religious faiths.

Anger is often a by-product of intuitive convictions about injustice, about unfairness. We feel ourselves badly treated, we see others slighted or ignored, and anger spurs us to try to improve the situation.

Envy and covetousness have, at their roots, an entirely defensible desire for self-improvement. For change. Even cows, contentedly browsing in the sun, will seek the greenest grass to munch on. Once, I watched a cow stretching its neck through a barbed wire fence, straining against the puncturing tines, to reach just a fraction further into the next field, where the long grass had not yet been cropped short.

The desire to do better is intrinsic to being human. (Indeed, I suspect that the message constantly relayed to current generations of young people, that they *cannot* expect to do better than their parents, financially and socially, provokes a kind of nihilism that contributes to much of the violence and vandalism endemic in our society today.)

"Doing better" needs a model. When we see someone who has "done better," those persons who have improved their lot in life, we tend to copy them.

The desire for self-improvement also lies behind our technological development, of course. But there's also something else – a willingness to risk, a willingness to invest in the future. Because we hope to relax tomorrow, we are willing to work harder today. The sin of *sloth*, as it was defined in the Middle Ages, was actually the rejection of this future-oriented ethic. While others sweated in the fields, or labored under an overseer's lash in royal building projects, the slothful person goofed off, confident that when winter came he would be sustained from the harvest of others' efforts.

Lust, of course, has its origins in the attraction of the sexes to each other. But that kind of attraction can be satisfied by a purely mechanical sexual coupling required for procreation. In some animal species, that's all that sex is. But not among humans. Somehow, an attraction initially driven by hormones provides a foundation for something more lasting, more satisfying. Two very different creatures, with different genes and different metabolisms and different reactions to their surroundings, can not only be attracted to each other sexually, but can actually like each other, can enjoy each other's company, can make a lifelong commitment to each other. Lust transforms into the wonderful feeling we call love.

THE TRANSFORMING POWER OF LOVE

My wife, Joan, and I saw the power of that transformation one winter, when we took a holiday in the Galápagos Islands. One afternoon, the group we were with stopped for a swim in the waters off a deserted crescent of red sand. But when some of us strolled down the sand towards the water, a bull sea lion lumbered out of the shallows toward us. He was in a bad mood. He bared his teeth. He growled. If we moved even a step closer to the water, he charged us, roaring.

It's not possible to reason with a ton of angry bull sea lion. We retreated. Hastily.

And then, out of the surf cascading onto the beach, his mate emerged. She was – at least compared to him – slim, sleek, and obviously sexy. Her presence transformed the hostile bull seal. In an instant, the two were rubbing noses and whiskers, coiling necks, whiffling in each other's ears.

The bull lost all interest in us, intruders on his domain.

Flipper to flipper, the male and female waddled together into the surf and disappeared.

Vices and virtues are always connected. Even among sea lions.

The
Seven Deadly
Sins

7

PRIDE

Everything that makes one person or group think itself superior to others.

I don't want even to suggest that the historic Seven Deadly Sins are the only sins we have to concern ourselves with. They're not. Later in this book, after I've gone through some of the groundwork that will help us recognize more clearly what a sin is, I'll look at some sins that I consider considerably more damaging – if only because they are largely unrecognized as sins.

But for the time being, the Seven Deadly Sins provide a reasonable lens through which we can look at our modern society. Now, as in the past, it is simply a list, an arbitrary selection of some socially harmful attitudes.

THE HEAD OF THE LIST

Let's start with pride, the sin that most of the compilers put at the head of the list. From Pope Gregory to Thomas Aquinas – when the list became more or less permanently established – pride came first.

They didn't call it pride, of course. As the intellectual elite of the Roman Catholic Church, they spoke and wrote in Latin. And the Latin word for pride is *hubris*. *The Oxford Dictionary*, the elite of dictionaries, defines *hubris* as "insolent pride or presumption...overweening pride towards the gods." *Hubris* has the implication of humans attempting to usurp the role of the gods, with the inevitable result, according to Oxford, "leading to nemesis." Not surprisingly, *hubris* is derived from the Greek word for tragedy. Challenging the gods was risky.

That concept also indicates why Gregory and Aquinas and others put pride at the top of their lists of Seven Deadly Sins. Pride not only lay at the root of the other sins, as Aquinas noted. Pride was also the only one of the seven sins that bordered on the ultimate sin: blasphemy, rejection of the authority of God. In that sense, it is a transition sin, a bridge between unforgivable atheism and the lesser, forgivable, mortal sins.

That must seem like an awful burden to load onto a bit of bragging. After all, every one of us has been guilty of pride, now and then. I treasure the letters I receive after I've written a book. I wrote *Letters to Stephen* about the grief resulting from the death of our son. Then I got letters telling me how it fitted the grief of an immigrant who had to leave behind her beloved Sri Lanka for the bitter winters of Ontario. And the corporate grieving of the staff in a large corporation who survived a massive downsizing. I knew I was writing about a universal emotion; I hadn't realized just how universal. And yes, I'm proud of insights I hadn't known I'd had.

But pride is a lot more serious than personal egotism. Self-centeredness, selfishness, arrogance, conceit, self-righteousness... They're not very nice terms. Because it's not a nice attitude. At the purely human level, it says, "Me first. I matter more than you do." At the divine level, it says, "I don't need you anymore. I am my own god."

To associate pride only with, say, bragging or boasting, limits and trivializes it. Pride underlies racism, sexism, ageism – not to mention slavery, bigotry, militarism and evangelism. All these have a common attitude: "I matter, you don't."

Pride is the foundation of almost all our "isms."

RACISM

Racism divides people by their skin color and ethnic origins. We're superior humans, racists claim – though they're not likely to express it that baldly in these politically sensitive decades. By corollary, of course, *you're* not as superior – if you're human at all. That's how, in the southern USA, blacks were invisible and expendable for 200 years. Grown men were called "boy," as if they weren't capable of higher development.

I've been told this story half a dozen times; I still don't know if it's true. According to the story, the biggest battle, since the Second World War, took place in Gander Airport, in Newfoundland. The US army had a platoon of black soldiers passing through on their way to postings in Europe. During their stopover, they went to the bar. When the bartender passed the first soldier his drink, he said, in typically friendly dialect: "There you be, bye."

Racism is not limited to skin color. Jews were visually indistinguishable from other Germans; yet that nation is now infamous for the most massive and best-documented genocide of our century. Bosnian Muslims and Serbs, Palestinians and Israelis, Indians and Pakistanis, differ often only in invisible ways. Religion. Ancestry. Patriotism. Yet the rivalry is so strong that it led to full-fledged civil war in Bosnia, to terrorism and recurring conflict in the Middle East. India and Pakistan have an active conflict only in Kashmir. But hostility still seethes so close to the surface that the two nations' championship cricket teams have not been able to play each other for years. Although they are considered the best cricket teams in the world, they were not able to have a playoff until this year, 1996, in a neutral country, Canada.

SEXISM

Sexism says that males are better than females. Or sometimes vice versa. But it's usually males thinking that they're better than females.

That gives them, they think, the right to abuse the women in their lives. To beat them. To let their anger rage out of control.

David Giuliano, a United Church minister in Marathon, northern Ontario, tells about counseling a man who admitted beating his wife. "I'm sorry, Rev," the man explained. "But I get angry, and I just can't control myself."

Later in the session, David deliberately provoked the man, who clenched his fists and got red in the face. "I oughta knock your block off!" the man growled.

"But you didn't!" David pointed out. "How come you can control yourself when you're dealing with me, but you can't when it's your wife?"

The answer is obvious. David Giuliano is another male, and a professional to boot. The wife is, well, *just* a woman.

That husband's attitude is far too common. I was shocked when Gilbert Lepine gunned down 14 women at McGill University, because of his anger at feminism. But I could still tell myself he was an aberration. He was not typical of men.

I have been dismayed as I hear about incidents of child abuse and wife beating. But I have been able to convince myself that the perpetrators were sick, disturbed, deranged. I could even ask myself why the victims stayed silent, or stayed in that situation at all.

But one day, while I still lived in Toronto, I flipped on the local news. It had five items on it.

❧ A 90-year-old woman was struck by several cars as she tried to cross a highway some 50 kilometers away from her home. No one knew why she should be there.

❧ Another woman was thrown out of a van. Then the van drove over her, several times.

❧ The body of another woman was found, stuffed into the freezer in her own home.

❧ Police were trying to identify the body of yet another woman, found floating in Lake Ontario at a waterfront park. She had apparently been dead for some time.

❦ A three-year-old girl had been abducted from a shopping center, but later returned home, apparently all right. Police were searching for the young man who had abducted her.

All five of the victims were female. Two of them were certainly the victims of male violence; the other three probably were.

For the first time in my life, I was ashamed to be a man. My eyes were opened to the propensity of males to violence – particularly, to violence against women. I'm convinced now that a majority of men consider women to be a lesser species. I don't really care why they feel that way. It may have something to do with misinterpretations of the story in the Garden of Eden, that God created woman from man, to be a "helpmeet," a helper, a companion, but clearly a secondary creation to man. Or it may equally well be that the Eden story was fabricated (or at the very least altered) to support a patriarchal and sexist attitude that already existed.

The reason doesn't matter. The fact, the action, speaks for itself.

AGEISM

Ageism – one of those wonderful new "isms" that defines a politically unacceptable sin of the week – glorifies youth and discriminates against their elders.

It has achieved legal status. The Human Rights legislation of most provinces in Canada forbids employers from asking about a potential employee's age. The legislation takes for granted that no one wants to hire a person approaching retirement.

When I was out of work and job-hunting a few years ago, a relocation firm told me not to put my age on my résumé. "Don't give them an opportunity to sort you out simply on the basis of your age," the counselors told me. "If they see your age before they get to your qualifications, they're likely to think that you're too set in your ways, or that you'll expect too high a salary for them to afford."

I was, at the time, 44 years old!

Ageism can work in reverse, too. A friend teaches elementary school. She came home one night with a long face. Her school board had announced, that day, that they would not renew the contracts of any teachers with less than 12 years seniority. "By next year," she lamented, "there won't be a teacher under 40 in our whole school. It will be filled up with burned out teachers waiting until they're eligible to collect full pensions. What kind of a stereotype is that going to set up for the kids?"

And where will the board find experienced teachers, when large numbers of older teachers all start retiring at once?

Though ageism has a new name, the sentiment has been around for a long time. When I was about 16, I went to a weekend conference of what was then known as the "Young People's Union" or YPU. Several of the organizers were my father's students, studying for the ministry. They were, I suppose, 21 or 22 years old.

When I got home after the weekend, my father asked how the event had been.

"Oh, fine," I shrugged.

He sensed some disappointment. "What was wrong?" he asked.

"Well, I thought it was for *young* people," I said. "But everything was run by these *old* guys."

Underlying all these examples is a kind of contempt for others, defined purely on the basis of chronological age.

SLAVERY

In our North American experience, we usually associate slavery with racism in the United States. But it goes back much further, and has a far more complex history. It's not limited to race. Remember the story of Joseph, in the Bible? Joseph was a smart aleck brat who drove his older brothers up the wall. He had delusions of grandeur, dreams that someday all his brothers would bow down and honor him. He got on their nerves until they sold him into slavery.

The *Roots* series on television, years ago, had a scene that still haunts me. Outside, a young woman was being flogged. Her screams echoed through the room in which the slave owner pored over his Bible with a magnifying glass, seeking insights into God's will for his life. If he heard her screams, he didn't pay attention. He wanted to know what God had in mind for the *white* human race, and for *him* particularly; she was neither white, nor, in his view, even human. She was simply an object, something he could own, a slave.

That's how pride evidenced itself in slavery.

BIGOTRY

Bigotry is intellectual pride. It presumes that I can understand this matter, and you can't. It often afflicts those who have had more education than others. Charles Emerson Winchester III, the surgeon from Boston on *M*A*S*H*, the television series that will probably air forever in syndicated reruns, epitomizes the snobbishness of those who have money, education, and privilege.

In our society, bigotry is often closely linked to racism or "class-ism," a ranking of people by their social class. Politicians and social planners despair of getting clearly articulated solutions from the working class people on whose behalf they develop policies and regulations. The National Rifle Association turns off any statement by anyone endorsing "gun control," whether or not the statement makes sense. Labor groups suspect anything that comes from management as being self-serving; capitalists disparage all socialists.

Robert White, then the head of the Canadian Auto Workers union, sat for a while on the board of Toronto's Skydome stadium. His protests about pricing, profits, and debt management were consistently brushed off by other board members, primarily drawn from the senior management of huge corporations and government ministries. They told him they had to deal with the "real world." Note the implicit reprimand. From their management perspective, they knew what the real world was; he, from his labor perspective, didn't.

White eventually blew up. In a front page story in the *Toronto Star* (I have to quote this by memory) he ranted: "They're talking about ten-dollar hamburgers and $500-a-night hotel rooms, and *they* want to tell *me* about the real world?"

I have been on both sides of bigotry myself.

On the one hand, I have been guilty, as an editor, of treating academics as incapable of writing in a popular style, or of meeting publishing deadlines. In those instances, I have failed to give them a chance to produce or to fail on their own merits. I have rejected them as a class.

On the other hand, I've had some of my own books rejected by a "Christian" bookstore. The store owner flipped to the bibliography at the back, saw a certain title there, and handed it back to the sales representative, saying, "New Age stuff. We won't handle it." He didn't even bother checking to see whether I had supported or condemned the "New Age stuff," whatever it was. In his eyes, it was enough that I had read the suspect text. He knew what was acceptable and legitimate; I didn't.

MILITARISM

Militarism drops any pretense of cooperation. With bare-knuckle brutality, it announces, "We'll do it my way." When military force is applied against a country's own citizens, it indicates that someone is unwilling to listen to a voice of dissent, no matter how reasoned that voice may be. Military force between nations reveals a breakdown in the will to negotiate diplomatically. Pride decides to ride roughshod over an opponent.

The military mentality may also pervade many organizations that have no overt connection to war. It presumes authority and obedience. The classic story – it has become part of our folklore – has a commanding officer dressing down a raw recruit. "When I tell you to jump," the officer barks, "I expect you to jump. You may ask, 'How high, sir?' on the way up!"

That military mentality shows up in businesses that expect junior staff to obey orders without question or criticism. It shows up in governments that stifle political opposition by imprisoning dissidents, as South Africa did for years. Or by executing them, as Nigeria did in 1995 with activist Ken Saro-Wiwa. Or by simply mowing them down with gunfire, as China did in Tienanmen Square and the US did at Kent State University.

It assumes that leaders must lead, and followers have no right to do anything but follow meekly.

EVANGELISM

Evangelism may seem like a strange item to include with all the others. But pushy evangelism is religious pride. Some people assume that they have a right to impose their faith, their answers, on others. People of other faiths, or of no faith, are fair game.

When I got my first job, I was paid by check, every week. The nearest bank was around the corner, one block over. A man used to lurk in the shadows at the corner, leaping out now and then to pounce on an unwary passer-by. He caught me a few times. As I waited for the traffic light to change, so that I could cross the street, a pair of long skinny hands would reach out of the crowd and grab me by the lapels of my jacket.

"Brother," he hissed in my face, "are you saved?"

I eventually changed banks to avoid him.

In lumping evangelism in with the other sins of pride, I fear that I may be doing an injustice to my ancestors. Both my parents, and my grandparents, were missionaries, charged with evangelizing – that is, teaching the good news of Jesus – to non-Christian peoples in India. They saw themselves as offering others something valuable, not as imposing an alien faith on anyone.

There is a difference. It's a bit like a running disagreement between two car owners. He, perhaps, drives a Chevrolet. I prefer a Mazda Miata. He likes trucks; I like sports cars. We can cheerfully dispute the relative merits of our vehicles. If his truck needs repairs more often than my car, I can point out the benefits of superior engineering and quality control. When I can't fit a large carton into my car, he can proclaim the values of a pickup. If either of us decides to switch to the other's choice, well and good. That's offering the other a choice. Evangelism sours, however, as soon as I start insisting that everyone should drive a Mazda, or he tries to force his truck preferences on others.

A UNIVERSAL PREDISPOSITION

Author and theologian Elaine Pagels, in her book *The Origin of Satan,* suggests that the whole concept of Satan is a by-product of

> how we perceive ourselves and those we call "others." Satan has, after all, made a profession of being the other... The social and cultural practice of defining certain people as others in relation to one's own group may be, of course, as old as humanity itself. The anthropologist Robert Redfield has argued that the worldview of many peoples consists essentially of two pairs of binary oppositions: human/non-human and we/they.

Similarly, British biologist Lyall Watson notes in *Dark Nature:* "This tendency to classify, to divide the world into 'us' and 'them,' members versus non-members, friend or foe, is one of the few true human universals... common to all people everywhere."

That tendency to divide, to make distinctions between ourselves and others, between "us" and "them," is a direct consequence of pride. Pride is, therefore, a universal malaise.

AND A SOURCE OF SALVATION

Yet, paradoxically, pride is also the means of healing many of these same social evils.

For generations, black people in the United States were told they were worthless, stupid, subhuman. Many of them believed it. They accepted their place as secondary to whites. That was a self-defeating situation. It could only change when blacks began to take some pride in themselves.

Rosa Parks started it. A black woman, tired after a hard day's work, she took a seat on a bus in Montgomery, Alabama, in 1955. A white person wanted her seat. That was the law – blacks could ride the same buses as whites, but they had to give up their seats to any white person. Rosa refused to give up her seat. She had enough pride to feel that she had as much right to that seat as a white person, whatever the law said.

Her refusal started a bus boycott, which grew into the civil rights marches that almost made Martin Luther King Jr. a saint. Black people began to feel some pride in their history and culture.

The new slogan was "Black is beautiful!" Until then, black had been a synonym for un-beautiful – for ugly, for sinful, for depraved... "Black is beautiful" was a symbol of pride. It was crucial to the social change that is still sweeping the US.

BATTERING THROUGH THE GLASS CEILING

A similar situation kept women in a subordinate role. They too had been treated for generations as second-class citizens. Until this century, both Canada and the US considered women too emotional, too unstable, to vote. In 1928, the Canadian Supreme Court ruled unanimously that women were not even "persons," and were therefore ineligible to hold public office. Fortunately, the following year, the British Privy Council reversed that decision, calling it "a relic of days more barbarous than ours."

But that didn't stop social researchers from ignoring women. When Piaget and Kohlberg did their pioneering studies on moral development, they didn't take account of women's experience. If women's experience failed to correspond to their conclusions, it was dismissed as aberrant. Women were simply faulty copies of men.

The Bible reinforced such distortions. The laws of the Israelites, established in the time of Moses, defined women as "unclean" during their menstrual periods (Leviticus 15:19–31). They had to isolate themselves from other women and from men. After menstruation ended, they had to ritually purify themselves, and be approved by a (male) priest, before they could return to society.

Unfortunately, vast numbers of women accepted these external definitions of their value. Many still do. They let their husbands or fathers or boyfriends speak for them and define what they should look like. They dress to please the men in their lives, even if those high-heeled shoes distort and permanently damage their feet. At home and at work, they don't think it's their place to make demands; they resign themselves to being overlooked and underpaid.

That situation began to change only with the rise of feminism.

It's not for me, a male, to comment on how far women have come since then. What I see as significant progress might be seen by many women as only token improvement. But I do think I see some significant progress. Today, women can be ordained as priests and ministers in most mainline churches. Only the most conservative evangelical churches and the Roman Catholic Church still officially exclude them from ordained leadership. In business, a small proportion of women have become executives. A few women have risen to dominate their horizons – Indira Gandhi and Margaret Thatcher come to mind. Yet many women still experience the so-called "glass ceiling" – an invisible barrier that limits their ascent in the corporate pecking order. Even today, the proportion of women in really senior positions is far lower than it should be, considering the number of women in the workforce.

The situation will change only as more and more women get enough pride in themselves, in their abilities, to batter their way through the glass ceiling, to demand that they be recognized for their own worth. And as more men give up some of their pride.

8
COVETOUSNESS

*The gimme-gimme mentality rides rampant
through all aspects of our society.*

Lf healthy pride helps to cure some
of the unhealthy effects of pride in our society, covetousness – greed,
avarice, desire – has become an essential element of society itself.

The old maxim, "Build a better mousetrap and the world will beat a
path to your door," is no longer true. Maybe it never was, except in
someone's dreams. Today's world is run by marketing. Gray's *Elegy in a
Country Churchyard* understood the situation only too well:

Some mute inglorious Milton here may rest,
Some Cromwell guiltless of his country's blood...

That is, says Gray, this rural cemetery may contain someone who had all
the language skills of Milton, all the leadership qualities of Cromwell –
but who never got catapulted to prominence. No one marketed their
talents. No one sold them to the public.

Marketing doesn't assume that customers will come in search of
Miltons, Cromwells, or mousetraps. You have to create a demand for
these products or services.

You've heard the cliché about sales reps so good they "could sell refrigerators to the Eskimos." There's an inherent contradiction there – why would people presumed to live in below-freezing temperatures need refrigerators at all? But the motivation for the sale is abundantly clear – they'll want refrigerators because they're convinced no home is complete without one. Or two. In designer colors.

UNREAL EXPECTATIONS

Once, while I was working for the United Church of Canada's national magazine, *The United Church Observer*, I visited the Caribbean to do a story about the social justice programs of the churches there. I saw examples of how church support had provided low-cost housing for poor people, had enabled family fishing boats to range farther to sea, had made marginal pig farms profitable, and had taught terracing to reduce erosion. I saw churches where exuberant worshippers raised the roof at every service, and churches where a few faithful members struggled to keep the walls up.

Regardless of the project or the parish, the most common problem cited was American television. Not the television evangelism, although it did almost universally promote a conservative and literalist theology pretty much incompatible with the views of the mainline denominations and their service agencies. Not the ads for luxury cars that cost more than an average household earned in five years and that would be hopelessly unwieldy on narrow island roads. Not even the propaganda for tobacco and alcohol, that created social and medical problems a struggling economy could ill afford.

The problem was the lifestyle that the *entertainment* programs took for granted. Television never showed a family living in a one- or two-room shack with a corrugated iron roof, with an outdoor kitchen, and air conditioning provided by a blow-through breeze. According to American television, everyone lived in a three-bedroom ranch bungalow with a stove and a refrigerator and a dishwasher, central heating, 2.3 blonde children, and a large shaggy dog.

Caribbean viewers now wanted the same things on their little islands.

Exactly the same thing happens to us. We're simply not as aware of it, because the contrast of lifestyles is not as stark. We see pictures of luxurious lawns, of glamorous cars, of exotic holidays, and we want to have them for ourselves.

TRAINED TO WANT

The biblical injunction says that you must not covet "your neighbor's house, you shall not covet your neighbor's wife, or male or female slave, or ox, or donkey..." (Exodus 20:17 NRSV). If I were a biblical literalist, I'd feel fairly comfortable with that commandment. Because I don't do any of those specific things. If that's a limiting list, I'm all right.

But remember that sins are attitudes, emotions, mindsets. Not wanting an ox or a donkey doesn't exempt me from the emotion of coveting. So yes, I admit it. I covet that black Porsche 911 Turbo with all-wheel drive that whistles past me on the highway. I covet the catamaran sailboat that glides effortlessly down the lake. I wish I could stop there. But I can't. I also covet a trip to Tahiti, a case of 16-year-old single malt Scotch from the Isle of Skye, and a beard with less gray in it. There is almost no limit to the number of things I can covet.

That's covetousness. Our entire consumer society is founded on it.

And no one is exempt. Because the advertising that promotes covetousness is so universal, and so subversive. It doesn't even have to be paid advertising. Car companies compete to have their products shown on the screen. From the grunge look to smartly tailored wardrobes, we take our clothing cues from the media stars we want to associate ourselves with. Travelogues show us pictures of Fiji or Samoa, where sandy beaches shine in the sun, where tropical forests dance with gaily colored birds, where translucent waves curl over into snowy foam – and we want to go there. Especially in February.

KEEPING UP WITH THE JONESES

In popular usage, covetousness and envy are often interchangeable. Dictionaries don't help a lot in distinguishing the two sins. To keep them clear in my own mind, I assume that covetousness refers to things; envy refers to people. I covet my neighbor's Porsche 911 Turbo sports car; I envy its owner.

Sometimes the two overlap. If I think of Sophia Loren as an object, something I want to possess, to show off to others, I covet. If I wish I could move in her social circles, with her self-confident assurance, I feel envy.

Covetousness, by my definition, means wanting something that someone else has. Covetousness deals with property, envy deals with persons; covetousness deals with having, envy with being.

Without covetousness, our whole marketing economy would grind to a halt. No one would care about "keeping up with the Joneses." If cars were nothing more than a means of getting from Point A to Point B, who would buy a Cadillac instead of a Chev? Without covetousness, we'd be content with what we had. We'd wear our clothes until they wore out, take vacations in our back yards, and never need to visit Toys Я Us®.

And no one would try to look like Madonna.

An acquaintance told me about his young grandson. "Can we get a boat, Dad?" the boy pestered his father. "Can we, huh? Pleeeeaaaase, Dad?"

Eventually the father gave in – it probably didn't take too much persuading – and bought a boat and trailer.

"Cool," pronounced the boy, staring at their new acquisition in the driveway. "Now can we go tow it up and down the highway like all the other guys?"

To that boy, it wasn't the usefulness of the boat that mattered. It was the having.

WHAT OTHER WAY IS THERE?

Another word for covetousness, of course, is greed. Or avarice. And pretty obviously, it's rampant in our society.

There is no question in my mind that I live in a greedy culture. What other word could I apply,

❦ when General Motors matches its announcement of the highest profits in history with the closure of two of its Canadian plants;

❦ when top executives inflate their own salaries while forcing thousands of former employees to live on unemployment insurance and soup kitchen handouts;

❦ when all five of the big banks in Canada make record profits (totaling in the billions of dollars, each), in the middle of a crisis of consumer confidence, with unemployment soaring – and immediately sharpen their pencils so that they can make even bigger profits?

The whole banking and investment industry is built upon greed. It's confession time again. I'm as guilty of greed as the next guy. In 1993, the employees of Wood Lake Books bought the publishing business that Ralph Milton and I had founded, 12 years before. For the first time in our lives, the Miltons and the Taylors had some wealth to invest. Investment agents came out of the woodwork. I chose one of them principally because of the service he gave me. Terry Dunn was the only one who took the time to work out in detail what kind of income those investments would yield for Joan and me over the next 30 years. But though I chose him for his service, when he comes around with his regular statements, I look them over mainly to see how much we've made this year.

I want the most I can get from my investments.

There may be people who invest in a company because they believe in the product, the leader, or the vision. There may be people who invest out of altruism, because their money might help the company survive. But if there are, I haven't met them. Everyone I know invests for the potential of return – either as interest, or as dividends, or ultimately as capital gains.

In fact, I rather suspect that most people, reading these lines, will shake their heads and wonder what I'm getting at. What other possible reason could there be for investing, other than to make the maximum possible gain?

Precisely. But can you call that motive anything but greed?

I like to think that I'm not particularly greedy myself. But perhaps I can afford not to be. That is, I'm quite satisfied with the house that Joan and I live in, for example. But it's a pretty nice house to start with. I don't know how I would feel in other circumstances.

COVETING FESTERS INTO ANGER

In Brazil, I once visited a squalid slum, a *favela,* beside a stinking sewer of a river. The people lived in shacks built from salvaged shipping cartons and advertising billboards. The water in the "river" was black, opaque, scummy. It stank. It was all they had to wash in, to cook with, to drink. They ate crabs captured from the mud along the shore. When the river rose, water came up through the ground, flooding their lanes and latrines.

On higher ground right next door, a wealthier member of society had built a mansion. With running water and indoor bathrooms. With airy balconies and broad verandahs to take advantage of cooling breezes. And with bars across the windows and broken glass on the walls around the property, to keep out the unwashed peasants next door.

I suspect that I would covet that lifestyle. I would envy that person. And the anger engendered by those emotions would seethe within me, day and night.

Thus does one sin lead to another.

9

LUST

If flour is a staple for the kitchen, lust is a staple for advertising.

When I was young and worked in advertising, the industry gathered in the Grand Ballroom of the Hotel Vancouver every year to view the best and the brightest of new commercials. Some were very clever. Some ad lines have become commonplace sayings. Ivory soap gave us "99.4 percent pure." Aspirin gave us "fast, fast relief." Certs taught us, "Two, two, two mints in one!" And do you remember, "I can't believe I ate the whole thing"?

Other ads deserved to be quickly forgotten. Chevrolet had a short-lived television ad that showed a car chasing a naked woman through a field of long grass. To this day, I don't understand the intent of that symbolism – except that a naked woman running through long grass certainly caught viewers' attention.

If flour is a staple for the kitchen, lust is a staple for advertising. Some evening, try watching the commercials instead of the programs. Dandruff shampoos, deodorants, hair coloring, tooth whiteners, perfumes, diamonds, clothing – all have one intention, to make you more attractive to the opposite sex. The commercials don't necessarily say so, of course. That might be a bit too blatant. The toothpaste will probably help your teeth. The exercise machines may improve your cardiovascular fitness. But let's not kid ourselves about the real intent behind bulging pectorals and flat bellies. It's not so you can stand and admire yourself in the mirror.

Just to ensure we get the point, the diamond ads end with the shadows of a man and woman kissing.

I'm quite confident that you have never seen any ad that says, or even implies, "Women will hate these jeans, and you'll look like a hayseed in them, but you'll be comfortable." And I'm sure you have never seen a women's perfume that's advertised "to keep men away."

Without that possibility of attracting the opposite sex, manufacturers of all these products would quickly go broke.

BAITING THE HOOK

As rising young writers of those commercials, we were taught that there were only a certain number of "appeals" that could "hook" viewers and listeners. There were a few fairly bland appeals, like thrift, or patriotism. Sometimes these conflicted. One minute I'd be writing a commercial for a Canadian-made shovel; it cost more than the imported shovel, but buying it supported Canadian jobs. The next, I was writing for another store that wanted customers to buy their imported shovels because they cost less.

There were some fairly powerful appeals, like pain relief, or entertainment, or enjoyment of good food.

But the appeal that always worked, we were told, was sex. It could sell anything from cars to casseroles. It sold shoes that distorted women's feet, cars that were accidents looking for a place to happen, and mechanics' tools. In the car shops I haunted in those days, the favorite calendar always displayed a busty woman and advertised Rigid Tools.

DELIBERATELY IGNORING THE TRUTH

We all know that over-indulgence in alcohol produces beer bellies, mental stupor, driving accidents, and sexual impotence. But alcohol, particularly beer, is almost always sold as something that will bring nubile young women flocking around brawny, wise-cracking men.

Perhaps it's what beer drinkers like to think happens. But it's far from a realistic portrayal. These commercials never show a bunch of bored, balding, pot-bellied men slowly drinking themselves into a stupor. They never show a group of kids puking their guts out in a corner of the parking lot. Or the hangovers that drag business productively down to zero that following morning. If it weren't for the occasional anti-drinking-and-driving promotions that stations carry as a public service, you'd never know that drinking can impair judgment and cause car accidents.

The reality isn't either appealing or sexy. But reality doesn't sell beer. Wishful thinking does.

MAKING CASUAL SEX THE NORM

Movies and television programs, the shapers of our standards, often seem incapable of recognizing motives other than lust. The person who *isn't* sleeping with someone else, nowadays, is usually a nerd, a geek, a figure of fun. It's simply taken for granted that the primary attraction between men and women is sex. I have watched stories where the woman's dearly loved husband is killed, tragically. She's grief stricken. But within a week, she has recovered enough to hop into bed with the person investigating the tragedy. Sometimes the same day.

That just doesn't happen in real life, in my experience. Grief takes time to get over; it is not simply set aside by sudden passion. After the death of her husband, Old Testament professor Vernon Fawcett, Ruth Fawcett told me she was going to grieve for him for a year. At the end of the year, she commented: "I had no idea how long these things take. I realize now, I'm only just starting to grieve what I lost."

It's a rare movie that acknowledges that a person in grief will not be ready for intimacy with anyone for some time.

If you believed Hollywood, you'd think that sex made the world go around.

I've been trapped by this seductive mentality myself. One day, I came out to my car, sitting in a parking lot. I had just finished fastening my seat belt and putting the key in the ignition when I noticed the woman in the car next to me.

She was very attractive: perhaps in her late 30s, neatly dressed, clear skin, and a magnificent mane of tawny hair. She too was fastening her seat belt and putting the key in the ignition.

She didn't start her car immediately. She fumbled in the briefcase on the seat beside her. And I caught myself delaying too, wondering if she would look up, if our eyes would meet, if we would sense some instant chemistry between us....

She looked up. Our eyes met. Nothing happened. Nothing at all.

With some shock, I realized I was acting like a twit.

I wouldn't know what to do with "instant chemistry," even if it had happened. I didn't *want* any "chemistry." I'm happily married, and have been for 36 years. I believe that relationships between people – like relationships with God – must grow and mature. Instant relationships are as phony as instant trees – plastic imitations.

I felt sick. I realized I had been suckered. In spite of all I had said and written, I had been taken in by a cultural obsession that expects instant cures for headaches, instant resolutions to international crises, and instant romances. I had fallen for the Hollywood myth, that somehow love will conquer all. Prince Charming will find Cinderella, Beauty will have her Beast, Rhett Butler will return to Scarlett O'Hara, and they will all live happily ever after.

Not very likely.

Years ago, Calgary writer Nancy Millar wrote, "Love is much too fragile an emotion on which to build a lifetime of marriage." By love, she meant the infatuation of initial intimacy, the sense of being swept off one's feet by someone else.

Roy Bell, Professor Emeritus at Regent College in Vancouver, shares that tough perspective. He has had years of experience in family counseling. Bell said bluntly, in an article in *Context,* the newsletter of World Vision Canada: "Romantic love doesn't last beyond 18 months."

Marriage demands something stronger, sturdier, like friendship. It calls for respect, support, loyalty, faithfulness. The Hollywood myth rarely gives more than lip service to those qualities, though. Lust is sufficient.

THE GENITAL OBSESSION

Our local soft-rock radio station occasionally plays a moldie oldie to keep listeners of my age from switching stations. The other day, in the middle of the usual mindless muddle of songs about youthful infatuation, they played an old Harry Chapin recording, about a father's relationship with his son: *Cat's in the Cradle.* It told of a father too busy with work to play with his son. The father puts off the boy with excuses – he's too busy, too many things to do, too many trips to take. But he makes promises: "But we'll get together then, son, you know we'll have a good time then."

At the end of the song, the father, now retired with time on his hands, asks when the son will visit him. The tables are turned; the son is now too busy for his father. With a shock, the father realizes, "He'd grown up just like me. My boy was just like me."

I always liked Harry Chapin's records. I never understood why until I compared them with current selections. Chapin's songs often dealt with what I think of as "the better" things in life. *Story of a Life* was about commitment and fidelity between husband and wife, each giving up some of his or her dreams for the sake of the other. *Taxi* recognized the worth of the person, regardless of the occupation. *Flowers Are Red* showed how a rigid school system can destroy forever the creativity of children. *Always Seventeen* both celebrated and lamented the great anti-war protest demonstrations of the 1970s. *Corey's Coming* told of the loneliness of a railway worker living down by the abandoned station.

For the same reason, I've always been moved by some of Vera Lynn's World War II recordings. She sang about hope: "There'll be bluebirds over, the white cliffs of Dover, tomorrow, just you wait and see..." She sang about sorrow: "I'll be seeing you, in all the old familiar places..." And she sang about ties stronger than death: "We'll meet again, don't know where, don't know when, but I know we'll meet again...."

By comparison, turn on almost any radio station today, and listen to the subject matter of the music. After that Harry Chapin record, I listened for over an hour, without hearing anything that didn't deal with physical sex – wanting it, having it, wanting out of it.

Banish lust, and disk jockeys would have nothing to play. The sin of lust has become a standard of the entertainment industry.

SOMEONE ELSE'S PROPERTY

Yet, strangely enough, genital sex wasn't the original focus of the sin of lust. Only *illicit* sex.

You see, however much I might dream about Sophia Loren, I can't have her. She belongs to someone else. So do I.

Much of our sexual drive is not about pleasure at all, but about possession. Did you notice what I said about Sophia Loren? That she "belongs" to someone else. That notion runs throughout our language. We talk about "my husband," "my girl," "my partner."

You probably remember the line in marriage ceremonies – fortunately it is not used much anymore: "Who gives this woman to be married to this man?" The question clearly conveys the sense of property and ownership. A few years ago, Mark Bedford, a United Church minister now retired in Victoria, BC, refused to perform weddings in which the bride was given away by one man to another. "I decided that I could not ask the question, about the bride, unless the groom also agreed to have me ask, 'Who gives this man to be married to this woman?' I never met a groom willing to be the subject of that question! It is loaded with connotations of chattel, ownership, and power over."

Possessiveness is so pervasive that I'm not sure I know any other way to speak about close relationships.

And that's the core of the moral rules about lust. Lust, in the old definitions, meant stepping over the boundaries. It wasn't so much sex itself that was the problem, but sex where you shouldn't be. The sin of lust has a lot more to do, historically, with trespassing on property rights than with passion.

Primarily male rights, of course. Biblically, women had no rights. If a pregnant woman was injured by an untended bull, for example, the bull's owner had to compensate the woman's husband. Not her. If a husband wanted to divorce his wife, all he had to do was say so, three times, before a rabbi. A woman without a husband or father was a nobody. Widows were lumped together with aliens and orphans – people who had no place in that society.

The custom of Levirate marriage protected, unintentionally, a widows status in the community. If a husband died, the dead husband's brother – and if no brother, then the closest male relative – had an obligation to marry the widow. It retained her status in the tribe. But she didn't have any choice about it.

In fact, even this protection was primarily for the male. The woman was simply a child-bearer. By marrying her to the dead man's brother, the tribe ensured that the tribal genes didn't fall into anyone else's hands.

DAVID AND BATHSHEBA

The story of King David's affair with Bathsheba is illuminating. The story itself is relatively straightforward. In his middle years, when he was beginning to doubt his manhood enough to stay home instead of lead-ing his troops into battle, David went up to his rooftop – and got the hots for a younger woman, Bathsheba, who was also out in the night air. The Bible says she was having a bath. In fact, say the scholars, she was prob-ably doing the ritual cleansing required after her menstrual period. David called her over to his palace and seduced her. Some say he raped her – certainly, she didn't have much chance to say no to the king. She became pregnant. Because her husband Uriah was far away in the wars, her preg-nancy would reveal to everyone that she had not stayed within her husband's boundaries. The penalty for straying was death by stoning. David could protect her by marrying her, making her his property. But he couldn't do that while her husband was alive. So David arranged for Uriah to be killed in battle.

Nathan, the prophet, had the unenviable task of telling David he had sinned. In a typically Jewish way, he did it by telling a story.

Once there was a man who had just one little lamb, which was like a pet. The rich man next door had lots of flocks, but when a guest came, the rich man took the poor man's lamb for dinner.

David was furious. "Show me that rich man!" he demanded. "I'll deal with him!"

And Nathan pointed the finger: "You are that man," he said (2 Samuel 12:7).

The story makes it clear that David's sin was not what he did to Bathsheba, but what he did to her husband. He stole the husband's prop-erty – first his wife, then his life.

STEPPING OVER THE LINE

The traditional definition of *illicit* sexual activity says nothing about feelings; it defines boundaries. The sin involved crossing those bound-aries, stepping over the line.

Jean Vanier, the founder of L'Arche homes for seriously disabled people, defines community as a place where people learn to live with their boundaries. "Everything about community is finding the right distance from people," he told a retreat in San Diego in 1990. A community, he suggested, is "networks of relationships, where people can find their space to live... without being destructive."

It's no coincidence, I believe, that the traditional wording of the Lord's Prayer, as it is used in most churches, defines our sins against each other as "trespasses."

On that basis, we should not limit the sin of lust to the sexual revolution at all. It's about overstepping bounds. Between individuals, and between groups of individuals.

In the last few years, Canadian churches have reeled under accusations of abuse in schools a generation ago. In Newfoundland and Ontario, the victims of abuses committed in Roman Catholic schools have brought charges against their former teachers. Charges of physical brutality, psychological oppression, and sexual abuse. Some of these charges have resulted in jail terms, some in out-of-court settlements.

Lord Acton coined a famous aphorism: "Power tends to corrupt, and absolute power corrupts absolutely." Isolated from home and parents, the pupils had no power; their teachers had absolute power. Apparently, that power led them to forget the proper boundaries between themselves and their young wards.

The abuse was, in some cases, sexual. But the sin was trespassing. Illicit lust led to overstepping the established boundaries.

In the western provinces, much the same happened in the residential schools for native children run by the Anglican, Presbyterian, or Methodist churches. (When the Methodists and most of the Presbyterians joined to form The United Church of Canada in 1925, some of their schools became the United Church's responsibility.) These residential schools operated from the 1830s for more than a century. The last one didn't close until 1984.

Today, years later, some native people are coming forward with charges of physical and sexual abuse. The mass media, as usual seizing on anything sensational that can be used to embarrass the churches, have typically portrayed the staff of these schools as uniformly evil. That has been very painful for many who dedicated their lives to what they genuinely believed was a worthy cause.

I have no doubt that many of those who served in residential schools were caring, compassionate, and deeply Christian people. I met quite a few of them during a period when I worked for the CBC on the northern British Columbian coast. They were, I would say, upright, honest, and self-sacrificing – almost to a fault. By conventional moral standards, they were exemplary.

The problem was not, in most cases, the individuals involved, but the system itself. The residential schools themselves were not in any way illegal. In fact, the churches operated the schools with government encouragement and financing. The schools were even well-intentioned – they aimed to remove young children from the supposedly harmful environment of their home villages, and to give the children the training and cultural conditioning they needed to assimilate into white society.

In the process, however, the residential school system did enormous violence to native children. By kidnapping the children from their culture, by refusing to let them speak their own language, by cutting them off from any experience of parenting, the schools created a generation trained to think of themselves as worthless.

The whole residential school system, in other words, trespassed. It violated boundaries that ought to have existed, to protect native culture, families, and communities. Within that larger systemic sin, a few people further violated proper boundaries between themselves and the students under their care.

The sin of lust, therefore, goes far beyond mere sexual hanky-panky. Illicit sex is merely the symptom. The sin – and the harm that the sin does – involves breaking the proper boundaries of human relationships.

10

ENVY

*To pull yourself up is a laudable desire
unless pulling yourself up means pulling others down.*

Ιf covetousness is about having,
envy is about being. You covet things; you envy people.

There's a directionality to these two complementary and often confused emotions. I think of coveting as being horizontal. That is, you reach
out and grab. You try to draw toward yourself your selection of desirable
objects. But you don't sense any need to change yourself or anyone else
in the process.

By contrast, envy is vertical. You reach up, to try to grab at someone
above you. And you pull down. Sometimes, by pulling down, you hoist
yourself up to a higher level, like chinning yourself on an overhead bar.
But sometimes, you simply pull the other person down to your level.

Or worse, you pull both of you further down, lower than either of you
was before.

There's a good side to all this. That is, envy – or jealousy, another
word for envy – almost always causes people to reach up. Envy intrinsically acknowledges that I am not all that I could be, all that I would like
to be. Therefore I reach up toward a model of who I think I could be.

After all, imitation is how we learn.

REACHING UP

When Dave Meier, the founder of Accelerated Learning Workshops, wants to get across the idea of an ideal learner, he shows a video of a small child trying to climb onto a sofa. The child falls over everything – a cushion, the dog, a toy – but keeps trying. The child gets part way up, and falls off. And tries again.

For young children, everything that happens to them is the foundation for new learning. They try to walk or climb, they fall down, and in failing, they learn what not to do as they try again.

Mostly, they learn from the adults around them. Because Daddy makes funny sounds, baby copies those sounds. Because Mommy stands up and moves around, baby learns to walk too.

And the practice continues as we grow and mature, though in less obvious ways. When I was first learning to be a writer, I copied other writers. (For a mercifully brief time, I tried to imitate James Joyce.) In time, without realizing it, I graduated to a style of my own. I knew I had achieved my own style when a participant in a writing workshop gave this reason for registering: "So I can learn to write like Jim Taylor!" (After such an accolade, how could I object to envy?)

But I've never seen anyone motivated by envy reach down. No one, in my experience, tries to drag themselves down to a lesser level.

Envy may sometimes *seem* to reach down. An aging executive envies the youth of a younger colleague; a repressed school teacher envies the uninhibited sexuality of a university student; an office-bound stockbroker envies the apparent freedom of a truck driver. But none of these persons really want to exchange positions. They merely want to add some new qualities to what they already have. So an out-of-shape university professor may envy the robust physical health of a mentally-challenged gardener. But that professor doesn't want to have the gardener's income, or working conditions, or ability to discuss philosophy intelligently; the professor merely wants the gardener's physical health to enhance her present lifestyle, to make it richer and fuller. If the professor is serious about improving her health, she will change herself for the better.

IF I CAN'T HAVE IT...

Another word for envy is jealousy. Which leads to spite. To rivalry, to competitiveness. And competitiveness, at its worst, says, "If I can't have it, no one else will." On the larger scale, this leads to the scorched earth policy pursued by retreating armies, who burn crops to ensure that their enemies won't find anything to eat, who burn cities to ensure that their enemies won't find anything to loot. Neither side considers the plight of the civilians; as non-combatants, they don't count. You saw this motivation put into practice when Iraq set fire to Kuwaiti oil wells during the Gulf War.

On a personal level, it's the motivation that led Mark Chahal to murder his estranged wife and seven members of her immediate family, the day before she was to remarry. That happened in Vernon, a city just 30 km from my home. If he couldn't have her, no one else would, either.

Fortunately, envy doesn't always go as far as mass murder. But let's not kid ourselves – envy is endemic to our society. Barry Sanders, a teacher, suggested facetiously on the CBC *Ideas* program that his whole profession is founded on "curriculum vitae envy" – the longest résumé gets the most attention. There's an obvious parallel to what Freud termed "penis envy." Regrettably, the program's participants had so much fun with that notion that they failed, in my opinion, to pursue the sin's pervasive seriousness in our culture.

Envy lies at the root of a philosophical problem historically known as the "Prisoner's Dilemma." The classic definition goes something like this: Imagine you're a prisoner. If you work cooperatively with other prisoners, you increase your opportunities to escape. But only a few of those cooperating will get out. On the other hand, if you attempt to escape on your own, you reduce your opportunities, but your chances of getting away with it are better.

Either way, you gain something, and you lose something. Which would you choose?

I heard a variation on the Prisoner's Dilemma on CBC's *Quirks and Quarks* radio program. Unfortunately, the program staff were unable to get me a transcript in time, so I have to cite this by memory.

A professor at Cornell University set up simulation exercises in which it was clearly to everyone's benefit to trust the other person. By working together, both persons could get a return of, say, 10 percent on their investment. If one person cheated, to gain a competitive advantage, that winner might get a benefit of 6 percent to 8 percent, and the loser would get only 2 percent or 3 percent. In other words, competing meant neither of the two would get as much as both would get if they cooperated.

Clearly, both ethics and profit dictate cooperation. You'd think everyone would see that. But a sizable number of students chose to compete, even though their choice penalized both them and the other student.

The professor tested students when they were just entering university. Then he tested them again after their first year of classes. The proportion of new students who chose to compete rather than cooperate was fairly consistent, whether they had registered for economics or for some other faculty.

In the second round of testing, though, something changed. Students taking a general Arts program, especially philosophy or ethics, were more likely to trust the other person than they had been a year before.

By contrast, those enrolled in economics were now about twice as likely (if I remember the statistics correctly) to cheat their partner – *even though they were better equipped to understand the benefits of not cheating!*

The results suggest to me that economic theory today has a hidden message. It teaches people to seek a competitive advantage over others – whether or not that course of action has any long-term benefit for society as a whole.

Consider some of the massive corporate takeovers of the past decade. From the perspective of a consumer, I don't see them creating any new products. I don't see them creating new jobs. I don't see them lowering prices. When The Bay took over Zellers, when Hollinger took over the Southam newspaper chain, they added nothing to Canadian society. These mergers did not improve my life in any way. Such takeovers do only two things. They inflate the Gross Domestic Product – not that I think that motivated anyone. And they eliminate an opponent, by taking control over it.

Economic theory is not always right. During the early 1990s, thousands of firms got rid of staff as if there were a sale on. But several studies during the mid-1990s indicated that things hadn't worked out as expected. Yes, firms that downsized did improve their short-term profits. But they did not, in many cases, improve their productivity, nor their marketing effectiveness. By contrast, firms that withstood the trend, that did minimal layoffs and cutbacks, grew significantly, both in revenues and in productivity.

In hindsight, cause and effect seem abundantly clear. It's hard to improve productivity when you get rid of your most experienced and skilled staff. It's hard to promote your company positively when you're terrified that the next knife may go into your back. It's hard to make intelligent decisions when you're suffering shock and grief over the loss of colleagues who have been friends for years.

THE TYRANNY OF FASHION

But for all the damage that envy does to business, I think its greatest damage has been to women. I say that with some personal bias. Last year, my wife Joan had to have surgery on her right foot. The joint of her big toe had disintegrated, and had to be fused to allow her to walk again without pain. The damage to the joint resulted, in part, from a genetic predisposition toward both arthritis and osteoporosis. But another factor, I'm sure, was the shoes she wore most of her younger years.

High-heeled shoes. That threw her weight forward awkwardly onto her toe joints. With pointy toes that bent her toes together. She wore them because she thought they made her look better. More attractive.

More like the models she admired in fashion magazines.

The fashion industry could not survive without exploiting envy. Or, for that matter, neither could the entertainment industry. We want to look like, feel like, act like, our favorite movie stars or models.

And so kids, on the sidewalk, play at the karate maneuvers they see Bruce Lee performing on the screen. Star Trek fans learn to speak Klingon, and imagine themselves aboard the *Enterprise*. A young man in our congregation knows everything there is to know about basketball superstar Michael Jordan. When our daughter Sharon was a pre-teen, she devoured magazines like *Tiger Beat*, to learn everything she could about the Partridge Family and other pubescent idols.

Sometimes, that envy makes us try to meet impossible – even dangerous – standards. Envy killed Karen Carpenter, for example. After a remarkable career as a pop singer, she died of anorexia. In a congregation we used to belong to, a young girl looked to me like skin and bones. At 11, she'd been through psychiatric counseling three times. She thought she was too fat.

Anorexia is simply the most obvious symbol of women attempting to be what they cannot be. They want to look as skinny as the models they see parading on television. The ultimate example of feminine shape is Barbie – the 50-year-old doll with big boobs and a tiny waist. *Discover* magazine, for its April 1996 issue, commissioned a physiologist to consider how much Barbie differs from a typical woman. It reported: "If a healthy attractive woman... keeps her hips the size they are, she would have to gain nearly a foot in height, add four inches to her chest, and lose five inches from her waist to become a life-size Barbie."

To retain her own height – a much more likely possibility – the typical woman would only have to gain about two inches in her bust, but she would have to lose about seven inches in her waist and perhaps five inches around her hips.

Barbie, to put it bluntly, is an anatomical freak.

Without envy, no one would even try to look like a Barbie doll. Without envy, anorexia would virtually disappear. Sales of all those elaborate contraptions that allow you to go rowing, jogging, walking, and cross-country skiing in the comfort of your rec room, would plummet. They're all based on envy, not need. And the ads play on that envy. They display lithe, muscular young models, who don't look as though they need the exercise. The ads never show a fat and 40ish male puffing on his treadmill, hair streaked with sweat. Him, I could identify with. So could most people. But they don't want to. They'd rather think of themselves as the Nordic god effortlessly striding along.

This is not a new phenomenon.

On a visit to the historic Gold Rush community of Barkerville, in British Columbia, Joan wanted to visit the seamstress' house. The sign said it was owned by a Mrs. Neates. I don't think the name was intended to be a pun. Joan loves stitchery and fabrics. While she examined the ancient equipment used in latter 1800s, I stood around. Most of the displays of women's clothing showed outer garments, layered with bustles and cloaks. Curious, I asked Mrs. Neates: "How many layers of undergarments did women wear under those voluminous clothes?"

She was delighted that someone should ask an intelligent question – "even if it had to come from a man." For the next half hour, she held forth.

I was amazed. They wore white stockings, held up by garters or a garter belt of some kind. Then pantaloons. Then slips or petticoats, often layered several times. (Women of lesser repute wore hoops. When the dancing or hurdy-gurdy girls wore hoops, the miners would try to "ring the bell" – that is, swing the girl from side to side, up and down, with her hoops swinging back and forth like a bell, until everyone had had a good look at her knickers. Better class women eliminated that potential embarrassment by not wearing hoops, and not dancing that way.) Over all that, women wore a full length skirt.

Up top, the basic garment was the corset. "Do you see the waist on this?" Mrs. Neates asked. "It's 18 inches. I often try this on small girls so that people can see that even children rarely have an 18-inch waist. But that was the size that fashion decreed was the ideal waist size. So from the age of eight, or 12, or 21 – whenever one had an 18-inch waist – this was buckled on and strapped tight, and from then on, it shaped the woman's body.

"Can you imagine what that squeezing did to the woman's internal organs and the muscles...?"

The bustle, and the large hip pads, were just another way to emphasize the narrowness of the waist. It increased the contrast.

According to Mrs. Neates, some women became so dependent on their whalebone corsets that they even wore it while bathing. They lost the use of their muscles. The corset forced kidneys and liver and reproductive organs out of place, making childbirth hazardous. Indeed, in some parts of society, Mrs. Neates said, it was customary, as soon as one became pregnant, to make out one's will.

Upper-class women, when they became pregnant, immediately retired from society. They couldn't possibly show themselves with expanded waists. Besides, without their corsets, they couldn't stand up straight, and the weight of the fetus made their back problems worse. Little wonder they spent much of their term in bed.

Envy, expressed as the social pressure to conform to fashionable standards, actually put upper-class families at an evolutionary disadvantage. Poor women, unable to afford corsets, were much more likely to survive childbirth. They still had gut muscles, and organs in the right places. "And more children," added Mrs. Neates. Probably healthier children, too, because of less trauma during birth.

FOOT-BINDING AND BODY-PIERCING

I'm sure that much the same arguments could be made for foot-binding in Chinese society, for filing teeth to points among Fijian tribes, for forcibly flattened foreheads among the Incas of South America, for body-piercing in North America. All are based on a desire to measure up to some external – and often unattainable – standard of beauty. They're based, in other words, on envy.

Without envy, we would have no fashion or cosmetics industry. And most orthodontists would find themselves – like tattoo artists, hair stylists, and the entire Partridge Family – looking for another line of work.

Envy is killing us. We can't live with it. But we can't live without it.

11

GLUTTONY

The pursuit, to excess, of any pleasure (not just food), constitutes gluttony.

Gluttony is not just about food. It also applies to drinking, and, by extension, to drugs, massage, tropical cruises – to any excessive pursuit of sensory pleasure.

At the time the early list-makers named gluttony as one of the Seven Deadly Sins, hedonism – the pursuit of pleasure for its own sake – was an option for so few people that naming it as a sin would have brought on gales of derisive laughter. Aside from the aristocracy and a few church prelates, life was hard. Most people were permanently cold, permanently hungry, and permanently weary. They slept on straw mattresses at best, more often on plain boards. They worked all day, at least six days a week, usually as someone's servants; if they had any time left over, they eked out a harvest for themselves and their families from a small plot of land. They lived in small, dark, overcrowded houses. Pleasure was a momentary thing, a quick gift snatched from the jaws of perpetual misery.

Most people in the past, in fact, lived at much the same standard as today's transients and street people. Their possessions were little more than what one of today's homeless wanderers can carry around in a supermarket shopping cart.

By contrast, most North Americans today – I'd estimate over 90 percent of us – live at standards that few of yesterday's nobility would recognize. Homes have central heating, or air conditioning, or both, to maintain comfortable temperatures year round. We may not all wear silks, but we have permanent press fabrics, synthetic fibers, and winter clothing that an emperor might envy. And any supermarket today would make our forebears' jaws drop.

So although gluttony is not just about food, food provides a worthwhile paradigm.

WHEN FOLKS GET TOGETHER

There was a time when a feast day meant eating well for a change. You slaughtered a lamb, and roasted it. You bought a turkey, or a ham, or a large chunk of beef. And you prepared it with all the trimmings: potatoes or rice, vegetables, salad, gravy, perhaps soup to start, fresh rolls and butter, and later, some sweet dessert to end.

You did all this because it was an exceptional situation.

At any other time, you might have one course. It was probably heavy on potatoes or rice, lean on meat. If you were fairly well off, you might have two courses: either soup or dessert to accompany the main course, but rarely both.

Most of the world still follows this pattern. Either the supply of food or the supply of money is too skimpy to allow much else.

When my father, W. S. Taylor, went out to India as a missionary, he took with him some Western notions of table manners. One of those notions expects guests to clean their plates to show appreciation to the host. In India, however, guests show appreciation differently. They leave some food on their plates, to indicate that their host was too generous – there was more than enough, too much to finish. In India, if you clean up your plate, it means you didn't get enough; you want more.

My father may have known this, when he himself was a child in India.

By the time he returned as an adult, he had forgotten.

He was taken to a small Indian village. The people were desperately poor. Even so, they considered it an honor to provide a meal for their guest. Dad sat cross-legged on the dirt floor of the host's house, while they served him a dish of lentil curry and rice. He did as a good Canadian boy should – he finished it off. He thanked his hosts.

They took his plate and headed outside. After a while, they came back with another plate of curry and rice.

Bravely, Dad tackled the second plate. It took some effort, but he finished it all too.

This time there was a definite air of consternation in his host's face. The plate disappeared again. And after a very long time, it came back with fairly small blob of curry, a small pile of rice.

At last, Dad says, he understood what was happening. He realized that he had probably eaten, in one meal, the family's entire supply of food for the next week. They might even have had to borrow food from their neighbors for his third plate.

When food is that scarce, a feast is indeed a special occasion.

To feast all the time was considered gluttony. And those who could afford it were usually punished by having gout, an excruciatingly painful affliction of the circulatory system, usually affecting extremities like the feet, a result of the richness of their diet.

OBESITY AS NATIONAL PASTIME

Today, in North America – I'm not talking here about the rest of the world – almost every meal would qualify as a feast just a few years ago. It's no wonder that the most common disease in the United States is obesity. And it's getting worse. Recent health surveys show that the Baby Boomer generation, which *ought* to know better, are generally in worse shape than their parents. They're both fatter and in poorer condition.

The prevalence of obesity does not contradict my previous comments about anorexia. Both are true. It's an indication that gluttony, lust, and envy are all out of control and fighting with each other for dominance.

It's one thing to pig out at home occasionally. Most people still impose some limitations on themselves at home, perhaps for financial reasons, perhaps out of nutritional concerns, perhaps just because, in today's busier and busier world, few people have the time to prepare elaborate multi-course meals every day.

But when people go out to restaurants, they expect a standard of eating that would have had King Herod drooling.

The wine steward stands by your table and asks, politely, "May I get you something from the bar?" You have a drink, an apéritif.

You order dinner. Perhaps an appetizer. Almost certainly a soup or salad. Then a main course. If it's beef, the restaurant may offer up to a pound of meat, 16 ounces of prime rib, sirloin, T-bone, New York steak… A filet mignon, at six to eight ounces of meat, looks pathetic on the platter. I've actually seen menus that describe a six-ounce steak or filet, derogatorily, as a meal suitable "for the smaller appetite."

I asked a waiter once, after we had been unable to finish our main courses, "Doesn't anyone else think your servings are too big?"

"Oh yes," he agreed. "Almost everyone does."

"Then why don't you provide smaller servings?"

He nodded. "Some restaurants tried that. They went broke. People want to feel that they're getting their money's worth."

Restaurants promote gluttony. Because we expect them to.

After all that, of course, the waiter stands by the table with his pad in his hand, and asks, hopefully, "Now, about dessert…"

Desserts – that's terminal gluttony. There are chains that serve nothing but desserts. There are chains that serve nothing but *chocolate* desserts.

I'm a sucker for desserts. I've driven 30 miles, across the international boundary into the United States, to have the mud pie at a restaurant in Bonner's Ferry, Idaho. It's enormous. The pie itself stands about four inches high and five inches wide – but it's hard to tell how big it really is, because it arrives buried in whipped cream, chopped nuts, all topped off with a maraschino cherry.

A nutritionist would probably tell me that there were more calories in that one dessert than Dad's Indian hosts had for a whole week.

And we are addicted to such excesses. At the now defunct Mr. Greenjeans in Toronto, I watched the people at the next table order a double chocolate brownie parfait. It came in a dish the size of a goldfish bowl. I was overwhelmed. I had to try one. So, it turned out, did six others of our party.

In Cochrane, west of Calgary in Alberta, during the summer, people line up for blocks to get into MacKay's, for what's claimed to be the best ice cream in Canada. A single scoop is huge. It's hard to eat a double scoop fast enough to keep it from melting and running down all over your hand and arm. Yet some people come out of that MacKay's with triple scoop cones. With a few raisins and a carrot, you could make them look like a snowman!

A SIN NAMED SUNDAE

A few years ago, Bob Ripley and I went to Haiti, to see firsthand the work being done by Compassion Canada, a church-based charitable organization. We met Haitians so anemic from chronic malaria that, by North American standards, they should be dying. But they had walked up to 25 miles, in burning tropic heat, to receive treatment. We scrambled over the terraces of tiny farms chiseled into steep hillsides. We lived for a week in a school run by Sister Joan, a Roman Catholic nun described by some as a living saint, where every pupil has lost at least one limb to disease, accident, or physical violence. We saw beggars picking scraps of rotten fruit from gutters. We watched pipes, driven through layers of rock and clay, bring water to arid villages. We saw people line up to get a precious bucket of water to serve a whole family for washing, cooking, and drinking.

The experience of poverty, of suffering, of deprivation, was overwhelming. We knew what to expect, and still, we were overwhelmed.

Our scheduled flight stopped in Miami. Bob and I took advantage of the stopover to head out to an ice cream shop. We sat in the warm, soft, Florida sunset and scooped deeply into our oversize sundaes, trying to banish memories of poverty.

I looked up from my sundae. "You know what sin is?" I said to Bob. "It's this sundae." I waved a hand in the general direction of Haiti.

Simultaneously, we pushed our sundaes away. We couldn't eat them anymore.

GLUTTONS FOR PUNISHMENT

But gluttony is, as I said earlier, far more than self-indulgence in taste. It is, in fact, any form of compulsive self-indulgence. And that includes almost everything today. Ours has, with good reason, been called an addictive society. Alcohol, tobacco, work, violence, drugs, gambling – you name it, there are people hooked on it.

What makes these things gluttony? The law of diminishing returns. As Bert Witvoet pointed out in an editorial in the *Christian Courier*, the pursuit of pleasure does not follow mathematical principles. Doubling your effort, or your expenditure, does not double your pleasure.

Witvoet used the example of a winter holiday. You take a one-week winter holiday to, say, the island of Aruba. It proves wonderful. So the next year, you go for twice as long. Or to twice as expensive a hotel. Or you attempt twice as many activities. Was it twice as good? Of course not!

If one ice cream cone tastes wonderful on a summer day, will two taste twice as good? Will four taste twice as good as two? "In the pursuit of pleasure," Witvoet wrote, "one plus one does not equal two."

Abraham Maslow, the psychologist, coined an assertion about human gratification. The closer one comes to gratifying one's desires, he said, the harder it is to do so.

People drink alcohol for pleasure – or forgetfulness, or whatever it gives them. Drinking twice as much enhances nothing. For anybody. The people who drink know that – intellectually. They know it affects their own health, their careers. They know it leads to violence, abuse, irresponsibility. Yet instead of drinking less, they drink more.

Gamblers lose money. Their solution is not to quit gambling, but to increase their wagers.

Workaholics admit they need to give more attention to their friends and families. They need a holiday. They need to take time to smell the roses. And they'll do it. Just as soon as they dig themselves out from under their current commitments. Which requires working even harder. More evenings. More weekends.

They are all gluttons for punishment.

That irrationality is a clear mark of an addiction. And it is not in any way limited to food. The drug culture is entirely based on the sin of gluttony. It depends on Witvoet's diminishing returns. The addict who simply has to have heroin, or cocaine, or LSD, or any other drug, soon has to have more, in the endless pursuit of pleasure which endlessly escapes him. But precisely the same pattern applies to anyone who simply has to have a massage, a manicure, or the latest computer game. The addiction is the same; the difference is only the degree of damage that results.

Remember that, the next time you hear about some man who beats his wife or murders his child in a fit of drunken rage. Remember it, when you hear about someone who loses her house because she spent all her income in a casino, or on lottery tickets. Remember it, when a gang war between drug dealers results in a shootout in a quiet residential neighborhood, leaving innocent bystanders crippled for life.

Remember that you're hearing about the sin of gluttony.

12

ANGER

The simmering undercurrent that fuels our contemporary urban society.

I was angry for 25 years. Not throwing-dishes-at-the-wall angry. Not being-nasty-to-everyone angry. Not even all-the-time angry. But a kind of slow simmering undercurrent of anger that erupted once in a while in too-tough memos, or in failing to treat people with the respect they deserved. I noticed it particularly in certain kinds of situations.

Traffic often brought this anger to the surface. I sat on what was supposed to be a superhighway, going nowhere. The car overheated and so did I. Prolonged committee meetings could do the same thing. So could dealing with bureaucracies of any kind.

It was worse at some times of the year than others. And I only became aware of this undercurrent of anger one year, on June 13. I was driving somewhere – to a committee meeting, probably – and getting very angry at all the other idiots on the road. I realized that this wasn't just a temporary emotion. For the last week, it seemed, I had been angry at almost anything: the tunes on the radio, my colleagues at work, an outdated computer... as though I was looking for a quarrel with someone, somewhere.

It was not an emotion I felt comfortable with.

I knew that none of the factors currently confronting me – the traffic, the radio, the meeting – could account for a feeling that had been growing for a week. What was there, about this time of year, I wondered, that had brought on this desire to lash out at something?

Then I remembered. June 13th was the anniversary of our family's move to Toronto, almost 25 years before. I had chosen to make that move, back in 1968, to further my career. For 12 years or so, I thought I had the best job in the world, working first as a writer, then as managing editor, for *The United Church Observer*. But somewhere along the way, I began to feel trapped in a city I felt no affection for. Our son's death there, of cystic fibrosis, at the age of 21, did nothing to enhance my love of the city. But other family concerns kept me there.

And gradually, I got more and more angry.

THE MOOD OF ANY METROPOLIS

That sounds like a petty illustration of anger. In one sense, it is. It didn't lead me to do anything violent, hostile, or, as far as I know, harmful to anyone.

In another sense, I think it reflects the mood of any large metropolitan area today. The environment generates anger. Anger becomes endemic. People feel trapped – in poverty, in dead-end jobs, in anonymity. They suffer with respiratory problems from urban pollution. Tensions rise with noise levels, with crowding, with changing population patterns.

Of all the families we knew well in Toronto, I can think of only two who told us they hoped to stay in the city when they retired. All the others planned to retire to a smaller town, or to their cottages in the country.

A big city almost needs a certain level of collective anger, I suspect, to keep functioning. It's what drives people to keep climbing those corporate ladders, to keep commuting an hour each way to work, to keep breathing the smog and the fumes. Suppressed anger fuels their refusal to give up in the face of the ever-increasing complexity of urban life.

I did some freelance work for the Canadian Cancer Society. At the time, it had its national offices in an office tower at Bloor and Bay Streets, reputed to be the busiest pedestrian intersection in Toronto. I could look down from the 17th floor and see a constant flood of pedestrians crossing the road, streaming around the cars stranded in the crosswalks, shouldering through the flow of people coming the other way.

"Isn't it wonderful?" a colleague gushed. "There's so much life, so much vitality going on all the time!"

What she called "vitality" felt to me more like impatience. Cars, unable to turn the corner against this unbroken parade of pedestrians, starting honking their horns half a block away. The people on the sidewalk didn't smile at each other, They didn't even look at each other. Somehow, without making eye contact, they tried also to avoid making any body contact. They moved like bottles on a conveyor belt: jostling, jiggling, but never joining up. They acknowledged each other only when two walkers got their shopping bags tangled, or when shoulders bounced off each other. Rather than saying sorry, they were more likely to snap, "Watch where you're going!"

Over the 25 years that Joan and I lived in Toronto, I sensed that driving styles became more aggressive, more hostile. People took more chances. They cut other drivers off more viciously. They made more middle-finger salutes, and shouted more imprecations out their windows.

I particularly recall one vehicle – a black Camaro with exhausts customized to make more noise – that roared past me at twice the speed limit. The driver gave me a finger. His girlfriend leaned far out the passenger's window to scream at me – and, I assume, at the entire line of traffic I was in – to "get the fuck off the fucking road." She wore a gold cross on a gold chain around her neck. She seemed oblivious to the contrast between her behavior and the symbolism of the cross.

In Los Angeles, I understand, drivers resort to guns so often to settle traffic grievances that the news media no longer bother reporting it.

"Violence appears to have become epidemic," writes British biologist

Lyall Watson in *Dark Nature.* "Mugging is now the most common of crimes involving physical force... No one in their right mind goes to the movies, watches television, or listens to popular music these days to get *away* from violence."

He goes on to describe the implications of this resort to violence: There are no traditional inhibitions, no biological or social restraints, no natural defences, against the gun, which turns every child into a superpredator with the power to kill at will.

All it takes now is the twitch of a finger... The principal culprit in this carnage is the handgun – 20 of which are manufactured every second in the United States alone, and put into 71 million hands and homes. Each of these instruments is designed, cast, calibrated, and sold with just one purpose, to end human life, which they do very well. There were 13,220 handgun murders in the United States in 1992, just 262 of which were ruled justifiable homicides in cases of self-defense... A million violent crimes a year are committed by handguns... In just three years, between 1990 and 1992, more Americans were killed by them than died in the entire seven years of the Vietnam War.

The suppressed collective anger of the city erupts less often in Canada than it does in the US. But it does erupt periodically. A picket line turns into violence. A school is vandalized. Thieves not only steal the stereo, they trash the house. Kids cut themselves off by joining cults and sects.

Kenn Ward, at the time a Lutheran pastor in a relatively peaceful Toronto suburb, was shocked to discover that students routinely brought knives and handguns to his children's school. He thought he was on good terms with his children. He was, after all, a minister, trained in relating to people.

But he discovered that his own children couldn't talk with him about the level of violence and drugs in their school. That information came out only when Kenn invited a local police officer to meet with his church youth group. The kids could level with the cop about what was going on; they couldn't with their minister. And certainly not with their father.

They talked about the time a boy came running across the playground, screaming, with a knife sticking out of his back. They talked about the kid who pulled a gun on a group. Most of them ran in panic; others left great skid marks in the grass with their cars, as they tried to corner the attacker without getting shot themselves.

"It was a real eye-opener," said Kenn, shaking his head. "Most of us have no idea of the kinds of pressures that kids are under today."

I haven't lived in a rural setting long enough to comment about it. But I suspect that our urban environments today could not get along without anger. Anger is the motivation for most of the adversarial activities of our culture: politics, sports, labor/management relations, the whole legal system.

FANNING THE FLAMES

When I was still a budding writer, I took a course from Raymond Hull, co-author with Lawrence Peter of *The Peter Principle*. Hull insisted that all plots depended on conflict: conflict with nature, with another human, or with oneself. That's why journalists thrived on stories about politics and sports, he said. Both subjects had built-in conflict – person against person, party against party, team against team.

Now and then I check out his theory against newspaper headlines. I think he's right, 99.4 percent of the time. Critics attack Shiela Copps over her GST promises. Michael Jordan crushes Grizzlies. Native blockade defies court order. Strikers reject final offer.

Even when there's good news, it's presented as an outcome of conflict. When school classes clean up the Don River valley, it's kids against garbage. When a government creates a new wilderness preserve, it surrenders to environmental pressures.

This is partly a matter of the journalists' mindset. When I worked for

The Observer, I covered a meeting of church and labor leaders. I wrote it up as "Church and labor still far apart." Fortunately, I showed my draft article to the late Clarke MacDonald, then head of the United Church's Department of Church in Society. "Jim," he said gently, "you missed the main point. The real news is not that they couldn't agree. It's that church leaders and labor leaders got together at all to talk about their perspectives."

But the emphasis on conflict results even more from society's expectations. A few years ago, *National Lampoon* ran some "good news" headlines. I can remember only two of them: "No one killed when subway train thunders into crowded station." And, "Family of five safe when wood stove doesn't explode." Thousands of planes take off and land safely every day; we pay attention to the one that crashed. Thousands of acts of kindness are performed anonymously in every community every day; we talk about the armed robbery at the local gas station.

Where conflict already exists, however, journalism fans the flames. Baseball could be considered a "gentlemanly" sport, most of the time. There's no hooking or spearing, no blindsiding or blitzing. The players usually treat each other with respect. But as the World Series approaches, sportswriters drag out stories of old feuds. Networks replay past humiliations. By the time the Series begins, the other side has become the enemy.

At the root of these expectations lies our compulsion to take sides, to identify ourselves by who we are against. Historically, this has been the Protestant position. Protestants were anything but monolithic. They disagreed among themselves over infant baptism, frequency of communion, the authority of scripture, and pacifism. They united on only one point – they were not Catholics. My father recalls his youth in a small Ontario town. Catholics and Protestants did not mix. They had separate schools, separate sports, separate parties. Catholics and Protestants didn't date each other, partly for fear of ostracism by both sides, but mainly because they had little chance to meet.

This compulsion to take sides can reveal itself in unexpected ways. In a denominational magazine, I read about a church leader strongly committed to the peace movement. But when his minister dropped in for a pastoral visit, she found him watching wrestling on television. And the viewer's body language revealed that he identified with the actions of the combatants in a way that contradicted his verbal commitment to non-violence.

BE A SPORT

Physical violence is the central core of most sports. Violence, as any number of battered women can attest, is the physical expression of anger.

The most popular spectator sports are the most violent ones. One January, Joan and I were on a cruise boat in the Galápagos Islands. Day-by-day, our group encountered sea lions frolicking in the surf, iguanas lazing in the sun, flamingoes stalking lagoon shallows on stilt legs, and blue-footed boobies imitating a swimmer attempting to walk while wearing plastic swim fins. The abundance of exotic wildlife overwhelmed us. Yet the most common topic of conversation at the dinner table seemed to be the Superbowl playoffs.

The more violent the sport, the more vehement its afficionados. The former owner of the Toronto Maple Leafs hockey team, Conn Smythe, made headlines by saying, "If you can't beat them in the alley, you can't beat them on the ice." Commentators professed shock, but Smythe merely stated publicly what everyone already knew in private – blood on the ice brings fans to the seats.

Hockey and curling are both played on ice. They're both highly competitive. There the comparison ends. In hockey, passions are permitted to erupt into violence. Hockey *legalizes* acts of anger – fighting, bodychecking, hooking, spearing – by specifying the precise length of penalty each act deserves. In curling, the only way to work out your aggression is to sweep the ice more vigorously. Guess which sport draws larger audiences.

Or compare fly fishing and football. Both my father and our daughter Sharon are fanatics about fly fishing. Every summer for several years, they arranged an expedition to some faraway trout paradise. You have to be a bit nuts to go in for serious fly fishing. Standing in ice-cold water up to your waist for hours on end, matching wits with a creature that has a brain about the size of your little finger nail, is hard to rationalize as pleasure. But it does offer a challenge. And that's an attraction that's easier to explain than why some 30,000 people would flock into a sub-zero outdoor stadium in late November to wrap themselves in blankets and shiver while they watch bull-necked football players attempt to injure each other on a frozen field. There's only one possible explanation for Canada's annual Grey Cup emotional binge: football is vicarious aggression, a kind of catharsis for the spectators' anger and hostility toward "the other side."

AN ADVERSARIAL SYSTEM

Sports has a lot in common with labor/management negotiations. The other side is always seen as opposition, often as enemy. The goal ought be a fair and equitable agreement, a mutually beneficial outcome. More often, the goal is to defeat the other side, to gain more than the other intended to give. As hard bargaining progresses, good intentions give way to anger and hostility.

Our whole legal system is based on adversarial relationships. Lawyers take opposing sides, with judges and juries as audience. The O. J. Simpson trial, lavishly televised, took the courtroom as entertainment to an extreme. In civil suits, this adversarial legal system often inflames already heated passions. Two friends of mine had reached a relatively amicable and mutually satisfactory settlement of their marriage separation. Then they took their agreement to their respective lawyers. Each lawyer wanted to get the most favorable result for her client. The ensuing hostilities – over a mere $1,000 difference – damaged relationships so much that the two were unable to speak directly to each other for over six months.

People go to court because of existing anger. Neighbors quarrel over an oak tree that drops its leaves on the wrong side of the property line. Drivers disagree over the causes and consequences of a rear-ender in a parking lot. The whole community is outraged over a rape or a murder.

SUBSIDIZING WAR

The legal system is at least a relatively civilized way of resolving that anger. In other situations, it erupts into war. In Bosnia, in Rwanda, in Kashmir, neighbors have taken the law into their own hands. With guns. And with mines, missiles, or machetes.

I haven't seen anyone attempt to measure the level of anger in the world today, but I'll take a guess that it must be increasing, based on the amount of killing going on. Project Ploughshares, an interchurch coalition dedicated to working for peace, estimates that there are currently 43 civil wars raging around the world. Only a decade ago, that figure was 37 civil wars. A decade before that, it was around 30.

The number of wars is increasing; so is the viciousness of the killing. North Americans have been appalled, in recent years, to witness on television the violence of the war in Bosnia, where former neighbors, living together uneasily for generations, turned on each other with long-suppressed hatred. We read with horror of massacres in Rwanda, where ancient tribal hostilities set Hutus and Tutsis against each other. Terrorism rocks Israel, as suicide bombers explode themselves in buses and shopping malls. Israeli forces retaliate. Arab boys develop uncanny skill at hurling their only available weapon, the rocks of which the region has an abundance.

The arms trade profits from this anger. The United Nations sent a peacekeeping force into Somalia to quell the conflict between tribal warlords there. Those forces found themselves under attack by their own weapons. When the former Soviet Union abandoned Somalia, thinking of Ethiopia as a richer prize, Western arms suppliers rushed in to fill the vacuum.

As I write this, Canada is still trying to sort out how some of its troops came to torture and murder a Somali teenager. I've read much of the news reporting about this inquiry. As far as I know, no one in that inquiry has noted that the soldiers were being shot at by weapons manufactured in their own countries. The jeeps that careered wildly through the streets, with machine guns mounted in the back, spewing lead indiscriminately at any imagined foe, came mainly from Western arms manufacturers. If I were getting shot at by my own country's bullets, I'm not too sure that I could remain cool.

More recently, in 1994, Canada increased its international arms sales more than 40 percent, mainly to Third World countries involved in internal conflicts. According to Project Ploughshares, Canada shipped $129 million of military goods to Europe that year; its sales to developing countries jumped to a record $342 million. More than half of those countries were cited by Amnesty International for "significant" human rights violations.

We subsidize anger, so that our arms manufacturers can make a profit. Through our taxes, we subsidize those arms sales. Our governments – wherever they are – provide the credit that enables violent factions to purchase sophisticated equipment to kill with. Teenaged boys in impoverished Somalia or Liberia, young fathers in Chechnya, cannot pay for machine guns and land mines out of their weekly allowances. Guerrilla groups in Afghanistan cannot pay for MiG jet fighters from sales of goat cheese.

Without anger, the arms trade would collapse. The military machine could be dismantled. Police forces could be minimized. And most lawyers would be out of work.

WHO ARE YOU VOTING AGAINST THIS TIME?

Politics, too, would be vastly different.

Before Joan and I left Toronto, the province of Ontario had an election. Voters were fed up. Particularly with Brian Mulroney's Conservative government in Ottawa. But also with David Peterson's Liberal government in Ontario. So they voted Peterson out of office. Given their mood, they'd probably have voted Mother Teresa out.

No one was more surprised than NDP leader Bob Rae, when the results came in, to find himself premier of a majority government.

And so it happened that Ontario – that bastion of big business – got a socialist provincial government. Business reeled. It was already in a slump; this felt like being kicked when you're down. Overnight, billboards of various kinds flowered, sponsored by previously unheard of business coalitions, opposing any and all of Rae's policies.

I was, at the time, teaching business communications for a local community college. One evening, I was invited to a meeting to discuss the college's continuing education strategy. I thought we were going to discuss teaching techniques or promotion plans. But the real agenda proved to be combating socialism. "We let those goddam socialists into office in Germany in 1934," growled one man. "And look what they did there."

It took me a while to realize he was referring to Hitler's National Socialist party, better known in its shortened form: Nazi.

By the next provincial election, the voters were still fed up – this time with Bob Rae's attempt to negotiate a "Social Contract" to cut expenditures on government offices and crown corporations. To replace him, they chose Mike Harris, whose Conservatives promised a "Common Sense Revolution." Clearly, the voters had little sense of what Harris intended; they just wanted Bob Rae out. Harris immediately set about dismantling by edict the social safety net that Rae had tried to reduce by negotiation.

And once again, the electorate was shocked. Welfare recipients and students felt the cut first. Civil servants came next. The whole nation watched on television as protest demonstrations turned into violent confrontations with riot police.

Citizens, it has been said, rarely vote *for* a candidate anymore – they vote *against* other candidates.

FUEL FOR THE FURNACE

Anger lies at the root of most public protests. Anger at logging practices in BC brought people from all over North America to blockade the
roads into Clayoquot Sound. Anger incited native bands to blockade themselves at Gustafson Lake, at Ipperwash, at Ganesetake. Anger fueled student protests during the Vietnam war, and anger drove Richard Nixon
out of office. Anger gave Greenpeace members the courage to sail their
boats into prohibited waters in Alaska, when the United States was planning to test nuclear weapons there, and into the seas surrounding
Mururoa Atoll when the French Government resumed nuclear testing.

Anger quickly penetrates political bullshit. In an earlier series of tests,
the French government brought politicians and scientists to Tahiti to
convince the Polynesian people that nuclear testing posed them no threat
whatsoever. Finally, one of the indigenous chiefs rose. "You have convinced us of the safety of nuclear tests," he announced. "We now believe
that it will be quite safe for you to test these devices in Marseilles harbor."

Substitute cool reason for anger, and politics might still work – though
it would be very different. Eliminate anger, and social protest would die
completely.

Anger is, in other words, intrinsic to our society. For good or for ill,
for preserving or upsetting the status quo, for stimulating or resisting
change, we cannot escape it.

13

SLOTH

If we weren't incurably lazy, would we have any technology at all?

One of my favorite cartoons shows a cave dweller, clad in furs, chipping away at a rock with a chisel and a stone mallet. "I don't mind the writing," he says to another fur-clad Neanderthal. "But oh, how I hate the rewriting!"

I'm writing these words with a computer. There is no reason why I couldn't write them with a typewriter. Or with a pen or pencil, on paper. Or, for that matter, why I couldn't chip them out of a rock, with a chisel. The words would be the same. Fewer, perhaps. But the same message.

I use a computer mainly because I'm lazy. I want to do the maximum amount of work, with a minimum amount of effort. The computer keyboard lets me work a lot faster than I ever could, pounding an old mechanical typewriter. In the same way, the typewriter let me create far more words per hour than I could with pen or pencil. The computer also makes corrections a lot easier. If I want to change a word or a sentence, I can do it without retyping the whole manuscript. In former times, with the old technologies, I often retyped an entire manuscript three or four times – every time that I found a few words I could improve. Or, if I felt lazy, I put up with a poorly phrased sentence just to avoid retyping it.

All technology derives, in a sense, from our desire to avoid unnecessary work. The horse, the bicycle, the steam engine, the car, the airplane – all of these enabled us to travel greater and greater distances with less and less personal effort. The sewing machine reduced the drudgery of hand stitching. In kitchens, the electric mixer eliminated the uncertainty of whether "beat until stiff" referred to the egg whites or the beater's arm.

The examples could go on and on. The telephone saved us from sending messengers with notes. The tractor allowed us to cultivate more land without using our own muscles to direct the plow. Electricity – besides giving us brighter light – freed us from filling lamps with oil and trimming wicks; it gave us heat that didn't require splitting wood or shoveling coal. The printing press let us read books without copying them out by hand. Flush toilets freed us from carrying stinking commode pots outside every morning.

Were we not incurably lazy, we would never have bothered devising the water pump or the cotton gin, the internal combustion engine or the public address system, the pneumatic drill or the central vacuum. We would never have invented the wheel – which simply helps us move loads more easily. Or such basic implements as the shovel, the hammer, and the axe – primitive as these tools may have been when cave dwellers first lashed a rock to a stick. An engineer explained to me once that the origins of European technological superiority over, say, African society began with the shovel. It enabled us to use our weight, coupled with the much stronger muscles of our legs, instead of our weaker arm and shoulder muscles, for breaking ground.

Sloth is, in fact, the motivation for technology.

INVESTMENT IN THE FUTURE

Now it's true that generating some of that technology requires an enormous expenditure of time and energy. The James Bay hydroelectric project in northern Quebec – if it is ever completed – will cost some $15 billion. It will redirect the flow of three major river systems. The first phase of the project alone required eight dams and almost 200 dykes, and flooded around 12,000 square kilometers of wilderness. All this effort produced about 7,500 megawatts of electrical power. To get another 12,000 megawatts will require further development on a similar scale. That certainly looks like a lot of work, for a lot of people. But remember why it's being done – not to create work but to reduce it. Someday, that power will enable millions more people to flip a switch somewhere and let a machine do a job that once required physical effort.

Alexander Graham Bell was probably one of the hardest working persons who ever lived. When we visited the museum dedicated to his inventions in Baddeck, on Cape Breton Island, I came away wondering how he ever found time to father children, let alone play with them. He made propellers out of his wife's venetian blinds, and kites out of her sheets. His best-known invention, the telephone, was almost an accidental by-product of his lifelong commitment to improving hearing and communication for the deaf. Yet every one of his hundreds of inventions was intended to reduce the effort needed to travel and to communicate.

When was the last time you heard of a wonderful new invention that requires you to expend *more* physical energy – to wash the dishes or the clothes, to send a message, or to drive to the store? Never, I'm sure.

THE SIN OF NOT CARING

If sloth is a sin, we're all guilty – every one of us living in any industrial or technologically developed society. We can't avoid it.

Today, sloth means laziness – the sin that welfare and unemployment insurance recipients are commonly accused of. Historically, it had a different meaning. When the Seven Deadly Sins were first defined in Greek, the word used was *accidia* or *acedia* – which means, roughly, apathy or indifference.

The sin was not caring. As the CBC program *Ideas* explained, "That emptiness, that not caring, became known as sloth from a Middle English word meaning 'slow'."

In fact, the two meanings come fairly close in the old fable of the ant and the sluggard. All through the summer, you may remember, the ant toiled away, gathering grain for the winter. All through the summer, the sluggard soaked up the sun and enjoyed himself.

"Better get your rear in gear," the ant warned the sluggard.

"Aw, I don't care," replied the sluggard, rubbing on some more sunscreen.

Then the winter came. The bitter winds blew. Snow covered the grain. The sun retreated behind gray clouds. The ant retreated to its nest, deep in the ground, snug against the weather, enjoying its well-stocked larder.

One day the ant heard a knock on its door. The sluggard stood there, shivering, with frost clinging to its back. The sluggard asked for food, for shelter. The ant turned the sluggard away.

The moral of this fable, of course, is that you can't expect someone else to feed you. If you don't care enough to make your contribution to society, you die.

Unfortunately, the supposed sin of sloth – whether defined as apathy or laziness – is used as a rationale for hard-heartedness. Bottom-line economists use it to justify cutting welfare payments to people who have too little income already. Tight-money governments invoke it to cut funding to artists and arts councils. Male-dominated institutions, religious and secular, use it to deny opportunity to women, to restrict income and recompense to those they class merely as "housewives" and "homemakers."

In the eyes of those who have power, status, and money, these folks are all sluggards. They fritter away their time on tasks of little or no apparent economic value. Housewives just look after the house and the children. Artists just splash paint onto a canvas. Musicians fiddle with an impossible sequence of notes on a stubborn violin until their fingers bleed. From the ant's perspective, these activities don't add any measurable value to society. Such pastimes become valuable only when a concert promoter can sell out a series of celebrity performances at $100 a ticket. Or when a painting is appraised at $1 million, and is likely to generate even larger capital gains for its owner in the future.

Suddenly, the sluggards have economic value.

There's a fable about measuring everything by money. King Midas loved gold so much that he was granted a wish. Everything he touched would turn into gold. His clothing. His garden. His food. His drink. His daughter. Old King Midas found himself in a lifeless wasteland, where everything was worth $400 an ounce, but nothing had value anymore.

FALSE PROPHETS

Unfortunately, penalizing these "sluggards" misses an important point in the fable. The sluggard didn't care enough about himself or the community to contribute to its labors. But the ant was also guilty of not caring. It was indifferent to the plight of another member of the community.

Politicians, economists, and corporate magnates are today's "ants." They think of themselves as prophets calling the people back to fiscal sanity. Their policies particularly penalize the poor, the uneducated, the handicapped and disabled in our society to reduce deficit financing. "Whether their analysis is right or not," commented a member of my church's small Bible study group, "they aren't the ones paying the price of their policies."

For that reason, however they think of themselves, they do not fit the tradition of the biblical prophets. The biblical prophets criticized their people. They challenged them to change their ways. But they also suffered along with their people.

In the Caribbean, I met a rarity – a professor of theology from Cuba. Uxmal Diaz taught Old Testament, the Hebrew Scriptures, in one of the few seminaries still operating in Cuba under Castro. He told me about Cuban people being forced to work in the sugar cane fields, virtually as slaves. "I could not protest about their conditions," he said. Not until he went out to the fields and worked with them. Not until he had shared their conditions, and their risks. Then, as a field worker, not as a professor with prestige, he could speak.

That was the biblical pattern. Even while Jeremiah raged against the iniquities of the Jewish people, while he warned them that enemy nations were about to conquer them and send them into exile, he invested in land. It was both a sign of hope in the future, and a symbol of solidarity with those who were going to suffer.

Elijah suffered drought along with the rest of the Israelites. Moses spent his 40 years in the wilderness, and never got to the Promised Land. Hosea knew, in his own household, what it meant to be jilted and rejected.

The prophets didn't stand on a mountain top – or a top-floor boardroom – and thunder down at the huddled masses below. They were part of the suffering masses.

Today? Here's what political commentator and former Conservative Party organizer Dalton Camp wrote in *The Toronto Star* (September 20, 1996): "A decade ago, taxes from corporations amounted to 25 percent of all federal revenues; today, that percentage is 6.7 percent. Why is that? Corporate profits are at record levels; where have the tax revenues gone? At the same time, personal income tax now makes up nearly half of all federal revenue."

That revenue from personal income tax is coming more and more from ordinary folk, not from the wealthy. That well-stocked ant's larder is now being replenished from the sluggard's shortages.

Not long ago, there was a report that a running shoe manufacturer paid more to a lone basketball star to endorse their product than their entire Southeast Asian payroll.

The ants have learned how to exploit the sluggards. And we act as if there will never be a winter.

RECOGNIZING CORPORATE SIN

A decade ago, when that corporate share of taxes was so much higher, Lynn MacDonald, then an NDP member of the federal parliament, addressed the annual meeting of the Canadian Church Press. She talked about sin.

Most of us, she said, if we met a starving person, would feel obligated to help. Many of us would give generously. "None of us," she concluded, "would take food *away* from that person." But corporately, she went on, that's exactly what we do.

The fact is that today in a global economy, everyone in North America lives on everyone else's labor. We are the affluent rich who reap the benefits of other people's toil. We sport carnations grown by Mexican peasant farmers with hand tools, broiling in the tropic sun. We swallow shrimp raised in ponds along the shores of Equador, artificial ponds that used to be wetlands lush with wildlife. We sweeten our coffee with sugar grown on lands seized from Brazilian peasant farmers, forcing them into destitution, despair, and grinding poverty. We wear clothing that cost a single mother her eyesight in a textile sweatshop in Thailand.

The basic trouble is that most us cannot think of sin without a sinner. As Lynn MacDonald pointed out: "Corporate sin is much harder to define than individual sin. It's easy to portray a murderer; we can picture the individual characteristics of the person and the act. It's much more difficult to recognize that most people suffer more from false advertising than from pickpockets, from drunk drivers than from murderers; and from industrial accidents than from rapes and muggings."

The problem with corporate sin is that we have no specific "sinner" to blame. Corporate sin reflects, she said, "the political will" of some group or body. It could be the decision of a select group such as a board of directors. It could equally well be the unexamined consensus of an entire nation.

MacDonald insisted that corporate sin needs to be recognized and challenged, just as much as individual sin does. If we won't tolerate lying or stealing by an individual, we shouldn't tolerate it in government or industry. Whatever it's called – "advertising" or "national security," perhaps – it's still lying. If we won't approve of individual murder, we shouldn't condone murder done in our collective name, whether it's called capital punishment or war.

In the kind of world we live in, we may never be fully able to apply Jesus' Golden Rule, to "do unto others as you would have them do unto you." But perhaps a partial application is possible – what we would not do personally to another person, we should not do corporately to our society, or to any other society.

The
Nature of
Sin

14

GOOD INTENTIONS

Things that end up as sins don't necessarily start off that way.

Good intentions chronically backfire. Or, to put it another way, sins almost always start off as good intentions.

In the province of Alberta, as CBC Radio's *As It Happens* reported recently, the Workers' Compensation Board thought it was taking a progressive step on behalf of workers by recognizing the risks of second-hand tobacco smoke. People with asthma and some allergies, for example, find their health and productivity affected by having to work in an environment where others smoke cigarettes, cigars, or pipes. If people affected by second-hand smoke received compensation, their employers would have to pay increased premiums. The WCB expected that their action would pressure employers to reduce smoking in the workplace.

But as it turned out, instead of encouraging a smoke-free environment, it's having exactly the opposite effect. One association of employers began recommending that its members hire *only* smokers, or persons willing to attest that they are neither offended by or affected by cigarette smoke.

So an effort to *protect* people afflicted by tobacco smoke ends up *penalizing* them.

It's a classic, contemporary, illustration of the paradox of sin. We do what we think is right; we find out later that it somehow went wrong. The rightness of the original intention does not ameliorate the wrongness of the eventual conclusion; the wrongness of the conclusion does not necessarily disprove the rightness of the original intention. Somewhere along the line, as Scottish poet Robbie Burns wrote more than two centuries ago, "The best laid schemes o' mice an' men gang aft agley."

The preceding chapters of this book lay the groundwork for an exploration of how this paradox happens. In the last seven chapters, I've looked at the historic Seven Deadly Sins, and how they affect us today. And you'll have noticed that same paradox contained within them. Not only do the traditional sins of pride, covetousness, lust, envy, gluttony, anger, and sloth still harm us, but we can't get along without them. The Seven Deadly Sins are also, in a sense, the Seven Essential Elements of our modern consumer society.

In Chapter 6, I suggested that every vice has, at its heart, a virtue. The sin of pride contains within itself the essential value of a healthy self-esteem. Envy and covetousness are the cancerous excessive growths of a healthy desire for self-improvement. Anger fuels the movement for justice; sloth is the drive for technological development. Beneath lust lies intimacy, the whole framework of human relationships, and the unconscious boundaries that enable us to live in harmony with each other. And gluttony has its roots in the very human desire to celebrate with each other.

No doubt there are many more sins that could be considered in our present North American culture. No doubt a number of those are as integral to its continued functions as these seven.

But for my purposes, those Seven Deadly Sins are sufficient as a matrix, a pattern, a means of understanding both the nature of the world we live in and the nature of sin itself. Through them, and what they reveal about the nature of sin, I hope that we – you and I together – can better comprehend and identify the sins of our time. For I believe that, just as we trivialize sins by restricting them to the personal level, we also

overlook a number of damaging aspects of our society simply because we
have not learned to identify them as sins.

BLINDED BY GOOD INTENTIONS

The main reason we don't see these harmful effects as sins, I suggest,
is that we're blinded by our good intentions. Deficit slashers in government will not back off; they believe they are doing something good for
society as a whole. Technocrats will not stop strangling a creative
company's artistic juices; they believe they are bringing necessary order
into chaos. At a much more immediate level, a father who routinely spanks
or beats his children will not see himself as abusing them; he will believe
that he's imposing discipline for the children's own good.

I do not believe that anyone consciously chooses to do the wrong
thing. That's a fairly radical assertion, and I need to explain it. "What
about the businessman who deliberately falsifies his accounts to avoid
paying taxes?" asked John Shearman, a retired United Church minister,
when he read that assertion in an early draft of this book. "What about a
trucker who keeps four logs instead of one to deceive safety inspectors?"
Yes, I agree. They know that they are breaking laws or violating regulations. They know that they risk penalties for their actions. But they did
not falsify their accounts or deceive the inspectors *because* it was wrong.
The did it *in spite of* their knowledge it was wrong – because they felt it
was right for them, at that time, in that situation. Or, more realistically, it
may have felt less wrong than the other options open to them.

They had, in other words, good intentions. John Shearman's hypothetical businessman lied about his income or expenses because he felt –
at that time, in that context, in his situation – that it was his best course of
action. He may have felt it was his *only* course of action. If he paid the
taxes required by law, he would have to lay off valued employees. Or the
bank would foreclose the mortgage on his home. Or he couldn't afford
to have his daughter's teeth straightened. He may simply have been

greedy; he may have felt that the government had no right to take that much of *his* money. Or, perhaps – I'm grabbing at straws here, I admit – he was a committed pacifist, who chose this circuitous way of withholding the portion of his taxes allocated to military expenditures. I don't know. But I believe – and yes, this is a statement of belief – that whether from principle or necessity or greed, that businessman does what he does because he is convinced it is, for him, at that time and situation, the best choice available to him.

I may disagree with his actions. So may you. But we view the situation from a different context. We have, perhaps, different values. We certainly have different experiences to bring to bear on our decision.

SEEKING THE LARGER TRUTH

There is a genuine danger that this view – the optimism that people choose to do what they believe to be right for their situation at that time – may lead at best to situation ethics, at worst to relativism. That is, that there are no right or wrong decisions. Everything depends on context and preference. I call an action wrong; you call it right; we can't agree, but we're each equally entitled to our own opinion.

I don't buy the relativism argument. I am not, decisively *not*, suggesting that all ethical matters are relative.

The question of relativity in ethics has a parallel in the question of truth. Is there one, single, absolute truth? Or does truth depend on each person's experience? In case of disagreement, I can simply say, "That's true in my experience," and you can't dispute my claim, because you have not had my experience. But is my truth really just mine, and your truth yours, and never the twain shall meet?

I have been helped here by reading about Mahatma Gandhi. At the base of Gandhi's theology was a lifelong search for Truth, which he equated with God (by whatever name). Gandhi realized that, being human and finite, he could never grasp absolute and infinite truth; he could only grasp a relative truth in a particular context. Through constant struggle with these relative truths, he believed, one gradually approaches the absolute truth.

That changes, for me, the significance of the word "relative." Instead of isolating truths or ethics from each other, it draws them together as parts of a larger and as yet unclear whole. The ethical challenge, then, is not so much to confront one person's notion of what's right or true with another view, but to find some way of assessing how closely each person's notion *approaches an absolute that we do not yet know.*

LEVELS OF MORAL DEVELOPMENT

It was just that assessment that Lawrence Kohlberg tried to develop in the 1970s. Other psychologists have since challenged some of Kohlberg's assumptions and methods. He based his studies exclusively on males, for example, virtually ignoring women's experience. Nevertheless, I find his insights helpful.

Kohlberg posed hypothetical situations that required his subjects to make either-or choices based on their current understandings of right and wrong. Here's an example. Suppose your child is seriously ill. You are unemployed and have no money. The drug store has medication that can save your child's life, but the pharmacist refuses to give it to you. Would you break into the drug store to steal that medication? Or would you let your child die?

There are many different possible responses to such a crisis. And it's worth noting here that women's responses differed dramatically from men's. Where men accepted the either-or, yes-or-no nature of the questions, women tended to look for additional options. Maybe they could negotiate with the owner of the drug store. Maybe they could work evenings to pay for the medication. Critics argue that Kohlberg excluded those responses from his data base, because they didn't fit his theoretical structure.

Yet, faulty or not, the structure itself intrigues me. Kohlberg ranked the responses he received, and the reasons given for those responses, into seven levels of moral development. They vary from pure selfishness at the lowest level to pure principle at the highest.

The responses might range something like these.

- ☙ I need it, so I'll take it.
- ☙ I'll take it, if I think I can get away with it.
- ☙ I'll take it, because it's for my family.
- ☙ I won't do it, because my family/friends wouldn't approve.
- ☙ I won't take it, because it's against the law.
- ☙ I'll steal it, because my relationship with my child matters more than anything else.
- ☙ I'll take it, because a system that denies life to an innocent child is unjust and unfair, and doesn't deserve my respect and obedience.

Each of those viewpoints reflects different values. Two people at widely differing levels of moral development may chose the same action – either to steal or not to steal the medication – but for dramatically different reasons.

Kohlberg, like me, takes for granted that each person will choose the action that seems most right to that person, at that time. You may personally reject some of those responses. So may I. That's because, according to Kohlberg's theories, we are only capable of comprehending and perhaps sympathizing with decisions close to our own level – possibly one level up or two levels down. A person committed to obeying the law unquestioningly may remember, without supporting, the feelings of a child who steals a cookie simply because he wants something sweet. That person can neither identify with nor comprehend the motives of a dedicated opponent of nuclear weapons who knowingly violates a court injunction against picketing a missile base.

I see Kohlberg's classifications acted out constantly around me. Take the real-life case of Maria Barahona, for example. Until 1980, she lived in El Salvador, where she campaigned against the military government of the time. Her life was threatened by government-backed right-wing death squads. The squads ransacked her home while she was in hiding; they beat and tortured a woman who had helped her, to try to find out where she was. In 1980, she fled to Los Angeles as an illegal immigrant. Ten years later, she came to Canada, where two members of her family had already been accepted as political refugees. In 1995, Canada's immigration department decreed that she must be deported back to El Salvador. She has five children, none of them born in El Salvador. Two brothers have been deported – both are now dead.

On December 6, 1995, on the eve of her deportment, Maria Barahona sought sanctuary in a church in Vancouver. As I write this, she is still there.

For some people, the issue is clear. The law is the law. If she's illegal, she must be deported. Others believe equally strongly that governments – whether of Canada or of El Salvador – must be obeyed. They take their cue from St. Paul, who wrote, "Let every person be subject to the governing authorities; for there is no authority except from God, and those authorities that exist have been instituted by God" (Romans 13:1 NRSV). Still others insist that human life is paramount; no government has the right to send a civilian into a situation that will almost certainly lead to her death. Others cite family values; the children will become orphans, deprived of their mother. A few hang their convictions on the historic separation of church and state, on the right of the church to grant sanctuary to victims of oppression and persecution regardless of what they may have done or not done.

These responses vary. But they all reflect, to some extent, Kohlberg's classification. Once you get past the most basic levels of response, which are purely selfish, all the responses reveal some kind of philosophical orientation. Everyone has a principle; the problem is that we don't agree on which principles take priority over others.

The significant factor for me is that Kohlberg shows how we change our minds on ethical issues. One view does not have to be wrong for us to move on to the next. Essentially, we graduate from one level to another as we learn more from our life experiences. So the small child who doesn't care about rules, who simply reacts to personal needs and desires, becomes the young boy playing street hockey who incessantly demands that everyone play by the local rules (whether they make sense or not), and then becomes the teenager who wouldn't dream of dressing differently from his friends but rebels against his parents' rules and ideals simply because they are his parents. Eventually, with luck, he (and remember that Kohlberg focused mainly on male subjects) will grow up to be an adult able to analyze and assess the reasons for the rules, and act accordingly.

The child did not choose to do wrong swiping a cookie – however much it may seem wrong to those at other levels of moral development. But a few years later, that same child may look back and realize for himself that he was wrong. That understanding always comes in hindsight, though, not at the time itself.

Kohlberg himself does not judge the rightness or wrongness of each person's response. He merely slots it on his scale. He focuses on the kind of response, not the response itself. But it's clear that, for him, the more principled the action, the closer it comes to absolute morality.

FOR THIS PEOPLE, THIS PLACE, THIS TIME

That position won't satisfy some people, I know. If they have a strong adherence to a conservative church, they're particularly likely to expect a hard-line, black-and-white distinction between right and wrong. I can only respond by pointing such people to a parallel in their own churches – the sermon. In a little book that unfortunately never achieved the sales it deserved, called *Encounters with the Bible*, linguistics professor Allan Gleason described the preacher's task:

> Each week he prepares by reading the biblical passages for that Sunday, and then asking himself, *What is the good news in these passages, for this day, this place, and these people?* (Emphasis in the original).

Preachers in theologically-liberal churches are likely to develop this theme, Gleason explained, using personal experiences, anecdotes, quotations, even humor. In more conservative churches, preachers are more likely to create a tightly woven fabric of doctrine, verse by verse. They rarely use non-biblical allusions. But despite this apparent difference in style, Gleason makes clear, the message of the sermon is always *for this day, this place, and these people.*

No one that I know of would argue that there is a single right sermon. Who would pay attention to a sermon intended for another people, in a different time, about an irrelevant situation? Sermons have to be right for *this* time, *this* place, *this* people. Such a sermon doesn't endorse relativism. It tries to be appropriate to the situation, while pointing to a more universal truth.

I think the same applies to ethics. To claim that people believe they are making the best choice, the right choice for them at the time, doesn't claim that their choice is right in either an absolute or a relative sense. It merely acknowledges their intentions.

And it explains their bewilderment when those intentions lead, later, to harm. To damage. To pain. When what they thought was right turns out to be wrong.

15

UNEXPECTED REVERSALS

A few insights from communications theory into the characteristics of sin.

How do virtues turn into vices? How do good intentions turn into sins? Theologians have spent centuries splitting hairs over such questions without, to my mind, coming up with any really satisfactory answers. I have found the most satisfying explanation not in theological niceties but in communications theory.

The best-known Canadian in the world is, in all probability, not Anne Murray, Robertson Davies, or even Wayne Gretsky. I think it's Marshall McLuhan – though I admit most of the people who've heard of him probably don't know or care that he was Canadian. Or, for that matter, Catholic.

Marshall McLuhan was, of course, the media guru of the 1960s and 1970s. More than 30 years ago, *Understanding Media* gave the world a whole new set of metaphors for understanding itself. Other books – *The Gutenberg Galaxy, The Mechanical Bride, The Medium Is the Message* – gave us "a pattern of insights into cultural transformation," in the words of *The Canadian Encyclopedia*. Some of his aphorisms, like the "global village," have become part of our daily speech.

Marshall McLuhan had the kind of intuitive, fertile mind that could snatch new concepts out of fog. Ideas and aphorisms burst forth as irresistably as grass thrusts its way through a newly blacktopped driveway. Journalists loved this characteristic – they could always count on a provocative quote or sound bite for their stories. Academics hated it – they accused him of being all flash and no fire. They accused him of being little more than a stand-up comedian, entertaining the masses with witty insights.

That criticism stung. At the time of his death, Marshall McLuhan and his son Eric were working on what they called the fundamental laws of media. I met Eric during the years when he was gathering together, sifting, and completing the mass of research that eventually became *Laws of Media: The New Science*, published in 1988 by the University of Toronto Press.

The McLuhans believed that they were doing for communications theory what Freud and Jung had done for psychotherapy a generation or two earlier. Perhaps even, in a smaller way, what Einstein had done for mathematics and physics. So they set about looking for the foundational principles of human communication, laws that could be as predictable as the law of gravity or the laws of conservation of matter and energy.

Because communication is a process, not an object, these laws predict processes, not products. They're not like the laws of chemistry, for example. In chemistry, if you mix, say, pure hydrogen and pure oxygen, and introduce a spark or a flame, you will get an explosion that produces nothing but water. If you mix hydrochloric acid and lye, you'll get a vigorous reaction that produces ordinary table salt. Things don't work that way with communications theory. If you mix a new element (such as printing) with an old culture (such as Europe in the 1500s) you won't get asparagus or cuckoo clocks. Rather, you get a new way of thinking, which today we define as literacy. You get a rejection of old patterns of faith, which we call The Reformation. And you create, strangely enough, a new and previously unknown disability that we call illiteracy.

Of course, illiteracy existed before Gutenberg. The vast majority of people couldn't read. But it didn't matter, because there was nothing for them to read anyway. Only the wealthy and the monasteries – which were themselves pretty wealthy – could afford to own hand-copied manuscripts.

So being unable to read was not a disability – it was normal. Not until printing presses made reading an option for everyone did an inability to read become a handicap. In that sense, then, Gutenberg's moveable type invented illiteracy.

The McLuhans found that there were four – and only four – fundamental "Laws of Media."

They also found that "media" covered much more than they had previously imagined. "Media" included not just radio and television and newspapers – it encompassed every form of human communication, including arts and crafts, manufactured products, and even social institutions. All of these, they realized, are ways in which we communicate with each other. When I buy a car, efficiency of transportation is only one of the factors that influences my decision. Much more important, often, is what I *feel* like in that car. How does it reflect the image I have of myself? We wear cars as we wear clothing; they are a form of self-expression, just like T-shirts and pink flamingoes on our lawns. Our whole civilization is a way that has evolved over generations and generations to enable us to relate to each other more or less harmoniously.

The term "media," in fact, covers everything that archeologists and anthropologists call "artifacts." (The McLuhans, for reasons of their own, decided to call these "artefacts.") In other words, every aspect of human civilization qualifies.

Including, obviously, sin.

THE FOUR LAWS OF MEDIA

Of the four "laws of media," three are irrelevant to a discussion of sin. Still, it's worth outlining them, so that you have the full picture.

The four laws can be summarized this way. Every new technology or process ("medium")

1. *enhances* some existing technology or process;
2. *retrieves* some previous technology or process;

3. *obsolesces* some existing technology or process;

4. when pushed to an extreme, *reverses* or "*flips*" into its opposite.

Obviously, that opposite is an entirely unintended result.

Here's an example. Superhighways were intended to *enhance* travel in cars. By eliminating crossroads and grid-pattern city streets, they *retrieved* old rural conditions when you simply followed a trail from here to there. They made traffic lights *obsolete* – at least on those superhighways. But when you push a superhighway to its limits, by cramming too many cars onto it, it *flips* into a vast linear parking lot. No one's going anywhere.

People recognize this truth intuitively, whether they have thought it through or not. Toronto has a freeway, heading downtown, called the Don Valley Parkway. Commuters derisively refer to it as the "Don Valley Parking Lot." At what's euphemistically called "rush hour," traffic slows to a standstill. Thousands of cars creep along so slowly that cyclists, even pedestrians, could easily pass them. Ironically, neither cyclists or pedestrians are allowed on the Parkway; highway legislation deems them too slow to keep up!

Here's another example. The computer on which I write this chapter has made my old portable typewriter *obsolete*. It has certainly *enhanced* the speed with which I can "input" my words, and the ease with which I can correct mistakes. But it has also *retrieved* from the distant past the scroll. The text flows in an endless stream up the screen and off the top, just as it did thousands of years ago when manuscripts were written on long rolls of papyrus or parchment.

And what happens when I push that computer beyond its limits? It "crashes." It overloads and destroys massive chunks of the information that I have so efficiently entered. It does the opposite of what it was intended to do.

Some people tell me that their computers stop being tools, and become addictions. They spend hours each day playing games, massaging their accounts, or surfing the Internet for information they don't really need and don't know what to with when they get it. Some have broken up their marriages to get together with partners they have only met on electronic chat groups. Unfortunately, I gather, their new partner often fails to be what he or she had seemed. While apparently enhancing communication, the computer restricted and distorted it; a vehicle for understanding flipped into a vehicle for *mis*understanding.

THE THEOLOGICAL APPLICATION

Marshall McLuhan was a devout Roman Catholic. Eric McLuhan still is. So, inevitably, the two McLuhans found themselves applying their discoveries to their faith. And they concluded that these "laws of media" apply only to *human* artefacts.

"Consider the lily," as Jesus once said. A lily is not a human creation. Therefore it doesn't retrieve anything, or make anything else obsolete. Nor does it enhance anything – except, perhaps, our appreciation of the scenery. But that appreciation is like the ancient riddle: if a tree falls in the forest, does it make a sound if there's no one there to hear it? Does beauty exist if there's no one there to see it? Does nature depend on humans for its validation? If it does, then that perception is itself a human artefact.

But most important, you cannot push a lily to its limits. And if you could, it could not flip into anything else. A lily just is.

A cloud, taken to an extreme, will never be anything but a cloud. Nor will a tree. Or an ocean.

But any human construction will, pushed to its limits, flip into its opposite. Take accurate spelling and grammar to an extreme, and they become pedantry that impedes communication. A social drink becomes anti-social alcoholism. Our toys become tyrants. Our possessions possess us.

We once lived next door to a neighbor who had a boat, a summer cottage, two snowmobiles, and a backyard swimming pool. "Jeez, Jimmy," he said to me several times each year. " I can't go to the cottage because I gotta clean the pool. I never get out in the boat because I have to mow the law and fix the roof at the cottage. I got thousands of bucks tied up in these things, and I never get to enjoy them!"

Far from bringing him the pleasure he had expected, his possessions had turned into prisons. He had hoped they would free him from the pressures of his urban life. Instead, they trapped him.

On the other hand, a daffodil, pushed to its limits, will still be a daffodil. It may become bigger or more colorful. But it will never become a septic tank. A rancid smelling, bad-tempered bear only becomes cute and cuddly when it is transformed – *by humans* – into a teddy bear.

OF GOD, AND OF HUMANS

That distinction between what's done by God and what's done by humans is important. Sometimes kids intuitively understand the distinction better than adults do.

Joan and I once had a small, happy and yappy, brown and white terrier named Mickey. Aside from his delusion that he could conquer every dog larger than himself, he learned well. We taught him a variety of tricks. He could beg and sit up, shake hands and lie down. If we stuck a wiener in his mouth and told him to "Wait!" he would. Most dogs roll over from one side to the other; Mickey did somersaults.

We were showing him off to a nine-year-old boy, one day. "Pooh!" the lad announced with contempt dripping from every word. "Those are all *human* tricks. Can't he do any *dog* tricks?"

Eric McLuhan and I debated his theories over several years. As a team, we taught business-writing skills to middle managers and civil servants. On long drives between Toronto and Ottawa, we tested and re-tested his "laws of media."

I was not totally convinced of his distinction between artefacts of human and of divine origin. A bubbling brook brings life to its banks. Taken to an extreme, it becomes a raging torrent, destroying everything in its path. A gentle breeze, taken to an extreme, turns into a tornado, a hurri-

cane, devastating forests and buildings. Small forest fires clear under-
growth, hasten decay, and enhance renewed growth; a big fire can rage
across half a continent, incinerating everything and leaving the land
scorched and barren.

Yet even in these instances, as Eric pointed out, the negative is a direct extension of the positive. The brook erodes more; the fire burns
hotter. There are no unexpected reversals.

Eric never backed down. "The laws apply only to human creations,"
he insisted. "You have yet to show me how anything that God made, taken
to an extreme, becomes its opposite."

VIRTUES FLIP INTO SINS

That leads me to a new understanding of the nature of sin. *Any human virtue, taken to an extreme, can flip into a sin.*

Try it yourself. Choose a virtue you value. Imagine what would happen if it became obsessive. Would it still be as lovable? As admirable?

Take thrift to an extreme, for example, and it turns into stinginess or
greed. Scrooge probably started with good intentions, just like most of
the businesses that downsized their most loyal staffs into the streets to
improve their short-term profit margins.

Neatness can become a fetish. Personal hygiene, overdone, turns into
squeamishness – about getting dirty, about getting involved in anything
that brings one close to the "unwashed masses." Unchecked coopera-
tiveness can make you a doormat to be exploited by anyone. Strength of
will can lead to tyranny; independence to machismo; friendliness to
intrusion.

Yes, I think it works even with love. Parental love, overdone, turns
into over-protectiveness, spoiling, dominance, the often-satirized "Jewish Mama" stereotype, the need to control one's children even when
they have grown up. In the same way, intimacy can easily transform into
possessiveness, jealously, lust....

A virtue, in other words, is never an absolute. It exists in relationship, in balance, with other virtues. It becomes a sin only when it becomes an obsession, when it is given unbalanced emphasis.

TOO MUCH OR TOO LITTLE

Greek philosopher Aristotle understood that, 23 centuries ago. He talked about moderation in everything. British author Lyall Watson commented, in his book *Dark Nature*, that for Aristotle, desires "become bad, and may be identified as wrong desires, if we want too much." And he continues:

> But – and this I think is Aristotle's most vital contribution to the discussion of evil, contradicting the schools of hair-shirt discipline which turn abstinence into a virtue – such desires may be bad and wrong also if we want *too little.*
>
> Aristotelian ethics is the ethics of "just enough."...Enough is enough, even of a good thing. Even moral virtues such as courage are good only if they lie along the narrow mean. A man who fears everything becomes a coward, but a man who fears nothing is a dangerous fool.

The limits to which one pushes a virtue to turn it into a sin, then, can go *either* way – either too much *or* too little. Doting parents who want to ensure they don't spoil an only child can end up giving the child too little love. A belief in flexibility can evolve into too little planning, to chaos, to anarchy.

If these examples seem trivial, consider the corollary: *"The greater and better the virtue, the more terrible it's going to be if it goes wrong."* Those are not my words. I wish I could claim them, but they came from Lady Helen Oppenheimer, writer and moral philosopher, on the CBC program *Ideas.* She went on: "It is the glorious qualities of human beings which are (most) corruptible...."

An old Latin maxim encapsulated this wisdom. *Corruptio optimi pessisma.* That is, "When the best is corrupted, it becomes the worst."

Obviously, the McLuhans' fourth law of media, that virtues pushed to an extreme can flip unexpectedly into vices, is not a new insight.

16

Shades of Gray

We can never know precisely when something good turns bad.

Presented with clear polarities, few of us have any difficulty knowing the difference between right and wrong, beneficial and harmful.

cleanliness	dirtiness
kindness	callousness
love	hate
food	famine
drink	thirst
beauty	ugliness
generosity	selfishness
gentleness	violence
loyalty	betrayal
commitment	apathy

Our problems come not when we try to distinguish between black and white, but between shades of gray. At what point does a shade change over from being fractionally closer to black to fractionally closer to white?

In printers' jargon, gray scales are identified by percentages of black ink applied to the paper. Pure black, of course, is 100 percent. Pure white puts no ink at all on the paper, so it is 0 percent. In between are an infinite range of shades of gray: 20 percent, 40 percent, 60 percent black, etc. There may, somewhere, be a light meter that can tell the difference between 49.99 percent gray and 50.01 percent, but I doubt if any human eye can tell the difference.

Just as we can never know precisely when a gray that is more black than white turns into a gray that is more white than black, so, I'm convinced, *we can never know precisely when something good becomes a sin.*

We recognize the change only when it has been pushed to an extreme. We can see it only when we look back, having passed over that indefinable line. We attain our wisdom only in hindsight.

THE PATTERN, NOT THE INDIVIDUAL ACT

The principle that we can never know precisely that moment of transition from good to bad, from helpful to harmful, from virtue to vice, has a couple of important corollaries.

First, you can rarely call any single choice or single action a sin. Sin grows in the *pattern* of choices, the accumulation of a number of acts that turn a virtue imperceptibly into a vice.

One splurge of overeating does not make you a glutton. Nor does one bout of overindulgence make you an alcoholic. A habit of overeating or getting sloshed does.

A feeling of unease in a roomful of people of other races or cultures does not constitute prejudice. A persistent refusal to associate with people who make you feel uneasy, a repeated denial of their worth and merit, does.

One outburst of anger does not make you a violent person. A repeated pattern of yielding to your emotions may.

No, I won't claim that one murder is excusable. Because murder, the ultimate expression of anger, is almost never an isolated action. It's the culmination of a habit of seeking violent physical solutions. (Cold-blooded murder, for either personal gain or perverted pleasure, might be the culmination not so much of anger as of envy, covetousness, or lust.) The men who shot and killed 14 women in Montreal, or 27 school children in Dunblane, Scotland, did not simply start spraying bullets spontaneously. They had nursed grievances for years. They had acquired their weapons. They had rehearsed their attacks. Even seemingly spontaneous deaths in bar room brawls occur only because of the combatants' ongoing acceptance of physical violence as a means of settling differences.

Nor will I suggest that a single extramarital affair doesn't really constitute infidelity. It may well destroy a marriage. But not because it's an isolated act. That romp between the sheets will only happen if the rompers are open to the romp. The affair itself becomes the last straw in a relationship already burdened by a prolonged pattern of thinking, of lust for other sexual partners. The long-term sin is lust; adultery is the consequence of the sin.

I can't speak for women, but I think I can safely say that almost all men occasionally have lustful thoughts about other women. Even so illustrious a person as former US President Jimmy Carter admitted to lustful thoughts in a *Playboy* interview. When do such thoughts turn the corner into sin? We can never know. The question is meaningless. We only know when they have gone too far, when they affect our actions.

IMPERCEPTIBLE TRANSITIONS

There isn't even a corner to turn. It's more like traveling around a very long, very smooth curve. You start off heading east, perhaps. The first deviations deflect you only fractionally from your destination. But as those deviations continue, you find yourself turning further and further – even though you may still be making some slight progress toward the east. But at some point, you'll find that you're no longer going east at all. You're headed back the other way. You're moving west.

The Hebrew understanding of sin reflects part of this reality. The root word, *hata*, basically means to miss the mark, as does the Greek *hamartano*. That is, in the example I just gave, you're headed east, and you get deflected off your goal. But the notion of missing the mark still implies that you know what you're aiming for. It doesn't explain how you can find yourself turned right around, going the opposite way, doing harm instead of doing good.

Another ancient biblical understanding saw sin as the other side of something good, like the flip side of a coin. If heads is good, tails is bad. Unfortunately, the image implies an abrupt change from one to the other. You have to flip the coin to get from heads to tails. Whatever the truth of the insight, the image reinforces the notion that sin can be clearly distinguished from righteousness.

A more accurate image might be a wedding ring, or a loop of paper. On the part closest to you, you see the outside of the ring. On the part farthest from you, you see the inside of the ring. It's the same ring. It's continuous. It's unbroken. You can't define exactly where you stopped seeing one side and started seeing the other. But the transition has happened.

DON'T BE TOO SURE

Second, recognizing that there are no clear dividing lines between right and wrong might make us a bit more charitable toward others. Too many of our squabbles presume that someone knows exactly the invisible line between good and bad, right and wrong, justice and injustice. The Inquisition presumed to know where that line was. Torquemada and his torturers presumed to know God's mind, God's will. The Inquisition might have avoided its own excesses had it realized that taking even the best of motives to an extreme pushes them over the line and turns them into transgressions.

I think of an acquaintance of ours. He was accused by his wife of abusing their children. He did spank them occasionally, he admitted. Not brutally, just enough to maintain discipline. He countercharged that she refused to discipline the children at all. Therefore she was teaching them to be irresponsible and selfish. Each parent presumed to know, definitively, where discipline turned into abuse or tolerance turned into neglect.

I maintain that we can never know that fine line. We can recognize only the extremes, not the transitions.

C. S. Lewis, author of such books as *The Screwtape Letters* and the *Narnia* series of books for children (and many adults), once commented that we all have a strange feeling sometimes of being aliens in a world that has gotten out of joint.

In my first book, *An Everyday God* (now, regrettably, out of print), I explored that thought a little.

What is it that tells us something is wrong? C. S. Lewis says it's God. Or, to put it another way, that sudden sense of alienation from the world around you is evidence that there is a God.

If there really weren't a God, you would never know you had made a wrong choice. Because if you're the final judge yourself, any choice you made would have to be right. Wouldn't it?

Sometimes it takes time for that realization (of something being wrong) to get through to us.

You don't imagine, of course, that a casual flirtation could lead to a messy divorce. It seemed harmless at the time.

You don't realize that a business sale to a foreign investor, or a large bank loan to an international corporation, might ultimately contribute to a branch-plant economy and to a loss of your own economic autonomy. It seemed like good business at the time.

Wrong decisions like these rarely show up quickly. But in the end, they always surface – when you find that your associates aren't the kind of people you would choose as friends, when you see your bad habits copied by your children, when national economic trends turn toward disaster, or perhaps when your life seems to be pointed more and more steeply downward.

Only in hindsight can we tell that we have stepped over the line. We discover after the fact that what we thought was right was actually wrong.

SUBTLE TRANSITIONS

According to an old Sufi tale, a teacher once asked his pupils to define the moment when night changed into day.

They thought long and hard about the question. Then one of them ventured: "When it is light enough to tell the difference between your sheep and your dog."

But that was not the answer the teacher sought.

"When you can see whether the tree over your head has oak leaves or maple leaves," offered another.

But that was not the answer the teacher sought either.

The fact is, night passes into day, and day into night, imperceptibly. There is a profound difference between night and day, but just as with sin, there is no exact moment when one can say, "Now it is day."

The seasons slip together the same way. In the temperate zones of the planet, where I live, there is a vast difference between winter and spring, between spring and summer, between summer and fall, and between fall and winter again. We all know that sudden sense of new life emerging; we know the heat of summer, the chill nip of autumn, the killing cold of winter. But none of us, watching the seasons turn, can say that at this moment, winter has given way to spring.

Granted, astronomers can tell us to the second when the sun passes over the equator in an equinox, or the precise length of the shortest or longest day. But the seasons themselves do not automatically change on those dates, like flipping a switch on a thermostat. Winter can, and often does, exact its last pound of flesh well after the spring equinox.

When the students had all offered answers, they asked the teacher for the correct answer. His reply shifted the ground. He told them: "When you can look into another's eyes and see there a sister or a brother, then you will know that night has changed into day."

17

THE SHOCK OF DISCOVERY

Sin is not something we choose,
but something we find ourselves already trapped in.

This morning's newspaper carries the story of a local woman convicted of stealing $110,000 from her employer to support her cocaine habit. The woman, says the story, initially stole small amounts of money from a local car dealership, always intending to repay it. But the unauthorized loans got out of hand.

I know nothing more about this case, nothing more about this woman. But in an odd and rather fortuitous way, the story encapsulates much of what I have been saying in this book.

The woman's *crime* is easy to name. Theft. Fraud. Embezzlement. Her actions are clear and easily defined by whatever labels you choose. But simply labeling the crime, as Karl Menninger pointed out in *Whatever Became of Sin?*, doesn't deal with the underlying sin.

Taking the first unauthorized ten dollars – or whatever the amount was – from her employer might have been a crime. But it's hardly a sin. Had she asked, her employer would almost certainly have said, Sure, take it. Just bring it back on Monday. If she had done so, if she had returned that money, she would not have committed either a crime or a sin.

But she continued to take unauthorized loans. Each one fed a pattern. Taking money became a habit almost as addictive as the cocaine she bought with her stolen cash. She started feeling that somehow, irrationally, she had a right to that money; she would never have to repay it. At some indefinable point, as expediency turned into habit, she crossed the line into sin. The sin of pride, I suggest. She began to believe that her needs, her cravings, took precedence over her employer's rights.

Of course, that sin was launched by another sin. Some would say that using cocaine was itself a sin. I don't agree. That first cocaine high may have been a mistake. It may have been a risk. But trying cocaine once is no more a sin than trying beer once, or having one cigarette, or one aspirin. But when drugs, alcohol, and tobacco become addictions, they push our self-control against the wall. They take over. They push our appetites for pleasurable sensations to an extreme that begins to harm us. And that sin, obviously, is gluttony.

The woman's sentence illustrates Menninger's contention that treating sin as crime misses the point. The judge ordered her to stay off drugs for two years, to do 100 hours of community service, and to repay her debt to the car dealership. But that sentence does nothing to help her conquer the sins of pride and gluttony.

BREAKING OFF IS HARD TO DO

Sometimes, it's possible to recognize a potential sin before you sink into it.

I arrived in Calgary one perishing cold winter night – it was -40° Fahrenheit, I recall – without a hotel reservation. I found the hotel and taxi telephones in the airport terminal. The first hotel I called had no vacancies. I was about to call a second hotel, when a tall, rangy guy in worn jeans and cowboy boots leaning against a nearby counter said, "I know a hotel that's got rooms."

"Are they clean?" I asked.

"Yup," he replied. "I can give you a ride inta town, too. Just waitin' for a friend a mine to show up."

He was as good as his word. The friend dropped us off at the hotel. I don't remember its name anymore. But the rooms were clean. And cheap.

"What can I do to thank you?" I asked the stranger.

"Let's go have a beer," he said.

So we did. We found we had lots to talk about. After a while, he said he had to go see another friend. But when he came back, he said, he could find a couple of girls for us for the night. "I'll meet you here, about midnight, eh?"

I nodded agreement. But I didn't show up. Perhaps he knew I wouldn't.

Having a couple of beers with a stranger may or may not have been wrong. Getting a ride with a stranger may or may not have been wrong. At least no harm came of either decision. But spending the night with a strange woman, prostitute or not, certainly would have been wrong by my standards. Even if I could have kept it a secret, it couldn't help affecting my relationship with Joan.

But most often, the implications are not that clear cut. The damage is done before you realize what you're getting into.

Sin, in that sense, is more like losing my wedding ring. A few days after our 36th wedding anniversary, Joan and I were working in the yard. The ring raised a blister at the base of my finger, a blister under the callous it had already created. When I tried to ease the pain of the blister, I discovered that I couldn't get my wedding ring off over my knuckle anymore. I'd gained weight since our marriage. Perhaps my knuckles had thickened with age, too. I realized I would have to have the ring stretched.

With a lot of effort, and considerable pain, I managed to get it off. But I didn't want to go around without a wedding ring. So I slipped the ring onto my little finger instead. It fitted reasonably well. It felt comfortable.

I should have gone to the jeweler immediately. I didn't. I just kept wearing the ring on my little finger.

Later that week, I took the dog for a swim down at the lake. We romped along the shore, and chased ducks. He got tangled up in some old pilings, out in deeper water. I swam out and freed him.

And when I dried myself, the ring was gone. It had fallen off my little finger. It was somewhere out there, in the black depths, down among the weeds and the rocks.

I went back the next day with snorkel mask and fins to search for that ring. I searched the bottom until I was shivering uncontrollably with hypothermia. I never did find it.

It's hard to pin down the point where I went wrong. When the ring slipped off in the water? When I went into the water? When I failed to go to a jeweler? When I put it on my little finger instead of leaving it in the bedroom? When I took it off?... The only possible answer is, any of those. and all of those."

The answer doesn't even matter. It's only when the damage is done that you even wonder about the turning point. It's only when the words are out that you wish you hadn't said them. It's only after you've been fired that you wish you'd been more punctual. It's only as you hit the guardrail that you wish you'd slowed a bit more for that corner.

CAUGHT IN THE ACT

Most of the time, we discover too late that we're mired in sin. Wisdom comes only with hindsight.

During the Depression years before World War II, King Gordon taught theology at United Theological College, on the campus of McGill University in Montreal. He came of a radical tradition. His father was Charles Gordon, a Presbyterian minister and armed forces chaplain better known by his pen name as novelist Ralph Connor. He used his novels to propound principles of ethics and social justice. After the 1919 Winnipeg General Strike, he was deeply involved in labor negotiations.

King Gordon followed his father's footsteps. Also ordained, he was a founder of Canada's socialist political party, the Cooperative Common-wealth Federation or CCF, which later became today's New Democratic Party. His theology reflected his socialist views. Eventually, his books and his radical views made him unwelcome at United College. This was, after all, a time which still tended to identify sin with playing cards or drinking rum. Gordon moved on to New York, where he became managing editor of *The Nation*. Later, he served the United Nations in Korea, the Middle East, and the Congo, before finishing his career teaching international relations at universities in Alberta and in Ottawa.

Sixty years later, we're just beginning to catch up to King Gordon's insights into sin. Basically, he said *that sin is not something we choose to do. It's something we find ourselves trapped in.* It's not something were tempted *into*, but something we're already *in*.

You realize with a shock, some day, that past actions, even well-intentioned past actions, have snared you in a sticky web.

Sin is like Wiley Coyote chasing the Road Runner. Wiley hurtles out into space, feet flailing away. He's halfway across the canyon before he realizes he has no ground under him anymore. Crash!

You only discover you're in quicksand when you start sinking. When swimming, you only realize you're in over your head when you try to touch bottom – and can't. That's the nature of sin, says Gordon. Real sin. Not the trivial little personal faults like missing church one Sunday or sneaking a smoke behind the barn. But systemic sin, the kind of sin that floods a whole society and carries us along with it.

Consider the parable of the snowflake. "How much does a single snow-flake weigh" demands one voice.

"Nothing, or less than nothing," replies a second voice, the voice of what economist John Kenneth Galbraith named conventional wisdom. "It cannot even be measured."

Yet as the snowflakes pile up on a branch, sooner or later, one of those snowflakes that weighs "nothing, or less than nothing," will be too much. You will never know which flake, too small to be measured, broke the bough. You will only know that the accumulated load was too great, after the bough breaks.

In the same way, King Gordon argued, the awareness of sin almost always comes as a shock. Something snaps, and there you are, covered in snow. Or something worse.

Gordon's context was the labor struggles of the 1920s and 1930s, when company owners and industrialists used all kinds of what we would now call dirty tricks to prevent labor unions from organizing. Gordon clearly took the union's side. But he did not assume that the owners and employers were necessarily evil. A lumber baron in New Brunswick, Gordon wrote, does not choose to be a union buster because he thinks it is wrong. He does so because he thinks it is *right*. He sees unions as a threat, a danger. They upset the historic order. They are taking away from him something he considers his, by right of ownership. So he fights against them, with all his might.

That's what makes him so dangerous – he thinks he is *right*.

If he really thought he was wrong, suggested Gordon, it would be possible to reason with him. It would be possible to show him other alternatives, which might serve both him and the union better. But because he is convinced that he is right, he can change only when he finds himself suddenly "convicted," brought to a different awareness of his actions.

LIKE A CONVERSION EXPERIENCE

The recognition of being trapped in sin comes like a conversion experience. The lumber baron, ruthlessly battling the unions with every tool available, thought all the time that he was doing what was best for the industry. And then something – perhaps a personal contact with someone harmed by his policies – opens his eyes. He's shattered.

A white resident of the southern US states doesn't think she's prejudiced. Indeed, she thinks she's unusually considerate of black people.

Suddenly, she realizes how even her kindnesses perpetuate a historical injustice. She's devastated.

At one of the first United Church General Councils that I covered as a reporter, I was assigned to a "sessional committee." About 20 of us sat in a big circle, discussing world development. Apartheid still ruled South Africa. Inevitably, we talked about economics. About corporate investments there. About purchasing practices here.

One man grew more and more frustrated. He could not understand what the rest of us were talking about. He didn't see how the products he bought in his local supermarket had anything to do with world justice. After all, *he* didn't support apartheid. *He* didn't keep black people in menial positions. *He* didn't deny them the right to vote.

It took him a long time to get the point.

"You mean," he spluttered finally, "that every time I buy a can of pineapple in the store, I'm supporting a racist regime in South Africa? That's ridiculous. You can't possibly spend your life examining every can of food to see where it came from and who benefits from it!"

But the fact is, from that moment of startled awareness on, that's exactly what he will do. He may not *want* to know who produced those oranges, or where that shirt was made. He may even avoid looking at labels. But he can never go back to a state of ignorance, of not recognizing that his purchases have international implications.

This "conversion" is usually sudden. It is always unexpected.

As a young reporter, I spent four weeks on an assignment in Malawi, in Central Africa. Officially, Malawi had no apartheid. Everyone, white or black or colored, was entitled to vote. In practice, the vote meant nothing, since the President, Dr. Hastings Kamuzu Banda, had declared himself President-for-Life, and ruled his poverty-stricken country with thinly disguised brutality.

Despite the official equality, however, many whites still thought of blacks as inferior, a sub-species of humanity. I was white, traveling with three black men, in a station wagon, to learn more about international mission work. The Dutch Reformed Church, the bastion of apartheid in South Africa, ran one of those missions. A gleaming whitewashed house sat in a valley, below a craggy volcanic peak that pointed at the sky like a melting ice cream cone. Jacaranda trees, fallen blossoms staining the ground purple, arched over the house's thatched roof. Around its windows, flaming red poinsettias grew wild.

The white missionaries welcomed me warmly. "Will you stay for lunch?" they asked, after showing the four of us around.

I looked around at my black companions. They nodded; we could afford the time.

"Do you have enough food on hand to feed four of us?" I asked innocently.

I didn't understand my hosts' momentary hesitation. It had nothing to do with the supply of food. It had to do with inviting black men to eat with them. I understood that only when I saw the missionaries' young children unable to eat even a mouthful of food during lunch. They stared, wide-eyed, jaws hanging open, at three black men sitting at their dinner table.

I learned later that no black person had ever eaten at that table before. In issuing their invitation, my hosts had assumed that my three black companions, whom they perceived only as servants, would forage for themselves. Or do without. My black companions, accustomed to the prevailing customs, made the same assumption. But when I innocently broadened the invitation, the missionaries couldn't withdraw it. The unwritten rules of hospitality to a stranger, and especially to a representative of a foreign church, took precedence over their prejudices.

To the amazement of the children, my black friends did not fit negative stereotypes. They acquitted themselves well. They knew how to use knives and forks. They conversed intelligently.

But the children's preconceptions were shattered forever.

I don't know how things changed in that home after that lunch. I do know that life in that home could never be the same again.

18

BELIEFS AND IDOLATRIES

The irrational reaction shows you when you have hit a nerve.

Ⅰf a conversion did take place in that missionary household in Malawi – as I believe it did – it was an accident. A combination of social customs worked in my favor. I violated one custom, out of my ignorance; they weren't willing to violate another, out of their commitment to hospitality. By accident, the whole situation did an end run around the biggest block to change.

Because sin starts so often with a good intention, people refuse to believe they're doing wrong. And I deliberately choose the word believe.

Sin always involves belief. If Torquemada, the Grand Inquisitor, had been reading this book, to this point he would probably shake his head in bewilderment. All this stuff about virtues hidden within vices, about laws of media, about taking things to an extreme, would strike him as so much circumlocution. But this principle – that sin always involve belief – would finally make sense to him.

Today, the Inquisition would not be tolerated. Amnesty International would condemn it outright, and organize protests. The United Nations would consider the Inquisition's methods a gross violation of human rights. From our perspective, its efforts to enforce correct belief on its victims may have been totally misguided – in fact, by taking those efforts to an extreme, the Inquisition itself crossed the line into sin. But in one sense, the inquisitors were right. The Inquisition recognized that all sin is in some sense a rejection of God. It gives the place of honor to something other than God.

THE GOLDEN CALF

You may recall the story of Moses going up the mountain to receive from God the Ten Commandments. He was up the mountain a long time. Maybe it took a long time for God to carve the ten laws into those stone tablets; maybe it took Moses a long time to condense into a memorable code the huge number of social customs that already existed.

Meanwhile, the Hebrew people waited at the bottom of the mountain. And they got bored waiting for Moses to come back down. They decided to take matters into their own hands. Lacking any understanding of a present God, they turned to past gods. They turned to the bull, worshipped for virility – in Egypt, in the Minoan civilization of the Mediterranean Islands, throughout the Middle East. Using the gold they had plundered from their Egyptian lords before fleeing into the desert, the Hebrew people made themselves a golden calf.

Even before Moses came down from the mountain, his followers had broken the first two commandments:

You shall have no other gods before me.

You shall not make for yourselves any idol, whether in the form of anything that is in heaven, or on the earth, or in the waters beneath the earth. You shall not bow down to them or worship them…
(Exodus 20:3–5 NRSV).

Moses, so the story goes, was furious. He smashed the tablets containing the Ten Commandments (Exodus 32:19ff). He smelted the golden calf down to ashes (which suggests that it wasn't very pure gold after all), ground the slag to a powder, mixed it with water, and made his cowering subjects drink the sludge. With the help of one loyal family, the first group to recognize the way the wind blew and to capitalize on it, he slaughtered some 3,000 of his own people.

Then he pleaded with God not to punish them anymore. They were, after all, God's people. If God destroyed the Hebrew people utterly, other nations might think God was incompetent. A supposedly almighty and all-knowing God wasn't smart enough to choose the right people. They'd think God had goofed.

So God simply sent a plague upon the people.

There are elements of high comedy in that story, as well as tragedy. But its central point comes through loud and clear – do not worship anything but God.

BEWARE OF WHAT YOU WORSHIP

The Inquisition took that command seriously. Over almost 500 years, with varying degrees of severity, in Italy and France and Spain, the church's inquisitors tried to root out any individuals who put their faith in magic, in science, in natural or supernatural healing. From my reading, they did not see that their own masters often put their faith in wealth, in status, in power. Perhaps they couldn't see that, because the inquisitors themselves shared that idolatry.

Others have also taken that command seriously. When I was growing up in British Columbia, the Doukhobor sect kept itself in newspaper headlines with its nude protest marches and barn burnings. At the time, media coverage leaned toward sensationalism, especially when it dealt with the most fanatical group, the Sons of Freedom. The most incomprehensible fact about the Doukhobors was that they were not guilty of arson. They didn't burn someone else's house or barn as an act of vengeance. They burned their *own* possessions. And they didn't try to claim insurance benefits afterward.

It took 30 years for CBC television's *Man Alive* program to offer a more balanced perspective. The Doukhobors were industrious. They worked together cooperatively. They prospered. But they recognized well – perhaps too well – how people could become attached to their affluence. So, as soon as someone seemed to place his farm, her kitchen, their wealth, ahead of God, they had to demonstrate their devotion by burning it down. And the whole community celebrated as it went up in flames.

We, outside the Doukhobor community, thought of their destruction of property as sin. They saw the sin as addiction to property.

Both views reflected beliefs. I won't presume to judge – yet – which was right. Because I haven't yet identified all the factors that I think are characteristic of sin.

But the fact that sin deals with beliefs – implicit or explicit – is crucial. And it explains why confronting people with sin, naming it, denouncing them to their faces, rarely works.

Another news item. A massive protest virtually shuts down Toronto. Thousands of people simply stay away from work. Thousands more picket government offices and agencies. They're all protesting the provincial government's slash-and-burn approach to welfare, social services, and capital funding. Premier Mike Harris promises not to be deterred, regardless of the level of protest, from his program of downsizing and deficit reduction. That's what we were elected for, he barks into a microphone, and that's what we're going to do!

As the preceding chapters have tried to point out, the people confronted by accusations of sin didn't think they were doing anything wrong at all. They probably thought that what they were doing was right. At least, it started out right. And anything they've done since then has been kind of forced upon them by that first decision. It has been consistent with that initial choice. So if that initial choice or action was right, how can what's happened since then have gone wrong? It must still be right! It must!

As King Gordon wrote, 60 years ago, people do not choose to sin. They discover that they are sinning. And they don't like it.

TOUCHING AN IDOLATRY

That's why so many people react with either shock or anger when accused of wrong-doing. The more they believe in what they're doing, the more vehement and irrational their anger.

Try telling medical doctors that their preoccupation with preserving life destroys human dignity and creates misery and suffering among the terminally ill.

Try telling a committed feminist that God is He.

Try telling sportswriters that their preoccupation with the win/loss statistics of the Montreal Expos – or the Edmonton Oilers, the BC Lions, the Toronto Raptors – has about as much redeeming social value as picking at acne pimples.

Try telling investors in money markets that international currency transactions reduce the welfare of a nation to a commodity. The collective hopes and dreams of a nation's people matter no more than pork bellies. Profits come at the price of lives.

For that matter, try telling an editor like me that spelling and grammar, facility with parallel constructions, and the proper use of the serial comma are meaningless conventions that matter only to pedants.

In all these cases and dozens more you'll get a reaction far out of proportion to the challenge. The reaction shows that you have touched a nerve.

In fact, you've done more – you have touched an idolatry. You've touched something they worship. Sports and language and economics are not just hobbies and interests – they become systems of belief. Everything – the meaning and purpose and value of life – hinges upon them. The people involved would not call these idolatries. In a few cases, they might admit to ideologies. They might agree that they subscribe to a system of convictions that they call capitalism or communism, feminism or ecology. But they would vigorously deny that they worship that system.

Fine. Ask the sportswriter to weed the garden and miss Superbowl. Ask the doctor to assist in a suicide. Ask a banker to authorize a personal loan at no interest. Ask an editor to disregard the difference between "it's" and "its." They cannot do it. They simply cannot.

I was at a media conference where the participants watched a video program on how US networks had distorted coverage of the civil war then going on in Nicaragua. It made the Contras look like heroes; it minimized or distorted the Sandinistas' accomplishments in literacy, health, and legal reform. The participants were outraged. There must be a way of allowing alternative viewpoints to be heard, they stormed.

Later that evening, one man unwisely referred to God "the Father." They shouted him down.

Alternative viewpoints were valuable, it appeared, as long as they were not alternative to *their* viewpoint.

But they, of course, could not see that.

19

FIGURE AND GROUND

*It's the parts of the picture we aren't conscious of that have
the most opportunity to influence us.*

When I was much younger, Maidenform Brassieres had an enormously successful ad campaign based on the slogan, "I dreamed I..." Women went walking, shopping, sailing, mountain climbing, sky diving – anything at all – wearing only a Maidenform Bra. Above the waist, that is. Because this was still a relatively prudish society, they were fully clothed from the waist down.

On the surface, it's a silly premise. Aside from Madonna, few women – and probably even fewer men – feel comfortable exposing their undergarments to public view.

But it's not supposed to make sense. Advertising works best when it infiltrates our subconscious. Our conscious minds know all too well that you don't save more by buying more; the claim works only when we *don't* think about it, when we allow it to become an excuse, a rationalization, however specious, for what we would like to do anyway.

It's like elevator music. You're not *supposed* to pay attention to it.

If we stop to think about it, we know very well that simply switching shampoos will not change dull hair with split ends into the kind of long and lustrous locks that that always swing in slow motion. As a 60-year-old male, I know that ordering a particular brand of Scotch whiskey will not cause nubile young maidens to drape themselves over me. A $1000 total-body-workout gym-and-rowing-machine is more likely to gather dust in the family room than give me rippling muscles. And I have no desire to drive a car onto the top of some rock pinnacle in Arizona anyway.

If I think about the content of these ads, I can only laugh at them.

But the advertisers don't *want* me to think about them. They want to slip their message into an unguarded corner of my mind while I help myself to another potato chip, or sip my can of pop, or place a long-distance call to tell my father that I love him.

Sin works the same way as advertising. It's most effective when we aren't consciously aware of what we're doing. More than that, *it depends on us not knowing what we're doing.*

In C.S. Lewis's insightful (and amusing) little book, *The Screwtape Letters,* Screwtape, the senior demon, writes to his apprentice, Wormword, instructing him how to lead humans into sin. The most successful way, Screwtape suggests, is to make people think they're actually doing good.

Communications theory – again – offers a clue about what happens.

It depends on the metaphor of "figure" and "ground." The terms come, by analogy, from painting. Imagine a picture of a landscape – perhaps an English landscape, by Constable. Within the painting, a solitary figure sits on the stream bank, fishing. A ray of light draws your attention to that figure. The more you concentrate on that figure, the less you notice the surroundings: the arching trees, the massing clouds, the delicate pattern of the artist's brush strokes, the canvas on which the artist applied paint, the color of the wall behind the painting, the good meal resting comfortably in your stomach… Yet each one of these factors influences your perceptions of that solitary figure, fishing.

Photographically, the "figure" snaps into sharp focus. Everything else fades into blur.

Yet the components of the blur are more than just "background." Some of them may be in the foreground. And others – like your meal –

aren't in the picture at all. Yet they affect how you see the figure.

The "figure" is anything you concentrate on, to the exclusion of the "ground." It doesn't have to be the human. It could be a horse, grazing along the fence. Or light, dancing on the ripples in the stream. Or the artist's technique. Even the frame that holds the picture. Whatever attracts your attention becomes the figure. The rest recedes into the ground. But the ground continues to influence you. You are simply not aware of its influence.

SEEING THE SPLASH, MISSING THE RIPPLES

Sin gets its power, its pervasive influence, from being invisible to us. If Wormwood's English parishioners had known they were being led into sin, they would have stopped. They would have backed off. Screwtape's strategy depended on getting them to focus so closely on the task that they couldn't recognize its implications.

It's like tossing a pebble into a pond. If you concentrate only on the splash, you'll never notice the ripples.

The sudden awareness of sin is like a sudden awareness of the ground, when what you had previously taken for granted snaps into focus. The man at General Council, the missionary children in Malawi, took their ground – their cultural environment and assumptions – for granted. It was a given in their universe. Suddenly, they become aware of a broader picture. A conflict, an unexpected situation, snapped the ground into focus.

That's how we discover sin. The ground, the surroundings, the environment, leap to your attention; the details you had been concentrating on fade away, and you see in a new way.

DOING IT DIFFERENTLY

Roger Bannister ran the first four-minute mile in history by being able to see the ground that others took for granted. Here's how it happened.

Since running records were first kept, the four-minute mile was considered an ultimate goal. Runners had come close, but no one had cracked the barrier. Some said it was beyond human capability. The four-minute mile became a mental block, as well as a physical one.

Until then, runners treated the mile as an endurance event. They ran marathons to get into condition. They ran on sand to build strength. They trained themselves for dogged determination. The mile was a killer distance, everyone thought. To conquer it, you had to build long-distance stamina.

I think it was Chris Chataway, who trained with Bannister and went on to become Britain's foremost track and field commentator, who explained Bannister's strategy. Bannister's idea, I remember reading, was to exhaust the total resources of the runner at the finish line. So he trained for the mile as a *sprint*. He trained himself to run as fast as he could for short distances. Then he kept extending that distance. When he could maintain full speed ahead for a mile before collapsing to the track, he had cracked the four-minute myth forever.

And suddenly, other people could run the mile in under four minutes too. Bannister himself faced challenger John Landy in the "Miracle Mile" at the British Empire and Commonwealth Games, held in Vancouver, August 1954. I remember that race as one of those milestones that mark key events in our personal histories – like the shooting of President John F. Kennedy, in Dallas, nine years later. Almost anyone over 50 can remember where they were, what they were doing, when they first heard the news of Kennedy's assassination.

The Miracle Mile was like that for me. I had just graduated from high school. I was vacationing with my parents – and a clutch of aunts, uncles, and cousins – at a remote fishing lodge in the far west of Ireland. The place had no electricity. Because of the time difference from Vancouver, the clan gathered around a battery-powered shortwave radio, late at night, surrounded by darkness. Had Rembrandt painted the scene, he might have called it Night Watch II.

We listened as Landy seized the lead in that Miracle Mile and held it until the final turn. Then he glanced over his shoulder to see where his opponent was. And in that momentary miscalculation, Bannister surged by on the outside to win. Our cheers rang across the bog, the little loch where the salmon leaped, the Atlantic surf pounding on the rocks.

Roger Bannister quit running soon after. But the breakthrough he engineered continued. Once the barrier was broken, other runners lowered his mark again, and again, and again.

Bannister's genius was not his physique. It was his ability to see the ground, where others saw only the figure. Obsessed with the four-minute barrier, other runners and coaches were unable to see that the training methods they took for granted had become a handicap. The figure blinded them to the ground.

THE DANGER OF INVISIBILITY

That is, I argue, sin's survival technique. *Most of the sins we get trapped in derive from what we take for granted.*

What we take for granted is dangerous to us, precisely because we are unaware of it. Because we are not conscious of it, we cannot do anything about it. Art Veldhuis, a United Church of Canada minister, visited his homeland of Holland during the 50th Anniversary celebrations of VE Day. "I attended various worship services," he wrote in *pmc: the Practice of Ministry in Canada*:

> They seem to be as puzzled as we are by the erosion of the church. Like us, they cannot let go of their churchy culture. They insist on gathering in their gothic buildings, singing their Reformation-type hymns, dressing their clergy in Genevan gowns, and worshipping as formally as any group of Amsterdam burghers in the Golden Age.
>
> The only exception was a special service with mentally challenged people, who freed others to sing heartily and laugh in church.

As an outsider, Veldhuis could see something that the Dutch church-goers could not. Their steadfast adherence to historic worship patterns meant nothing to anyone but them. To those they wanted to attract into the church, their traditions were irrelevant.

He could see the ground; they could only see the figure.

RELINQUISHING FREEDOM OF CHOICE

When we take the ground for granted, we allow it to dictate our decisions for us. That is the significance of two elements of the AA Twelve-Step program:

4. Made a searching and fearless moral inventory of ourselves.
5. Admitted to God, to ourselves, and to another human being the exact nature of our wrongs.

The fifth step simply forces one to do the fourth step. The moral inventory brings into consciousness one's wrongs. Otherwise, they can continue to do their dirty work undercover, unrecognized. They remain ground; they are never brought forward as figure.

And the ground is enormously influential. Even in the criminal underworld, a crook will do what the environment demands. Where compassion is scorned, no one in their right mind would imperil themselves by being kind.

In a world driven by the bottom line, no one will risk position and status by advocating a money-losing proposition that keeps people employed.

In a totally competitive environment, an athlete dare not back off to spare an opponent humiliation; that margin of victory could prove crucial later.

Seen from other contexts, kindness, generosity, or compassion might seem preferable responses. In these settings, the participants may feel they have no choice; they must, simply must, do what they must do.

Let's be more specific. Imagine a basketball team. They're all million-aires, perhaps, wearing expensive, brand name shoes stitched in a sweat shop somewhere in Calcutta. But they don't think they can do anything else. Refusing to endorse those products won't stop the exploitation of those women; it means only that someone else will get the endorsement fee. This night, they're playing a weaker team. They rack up an enormous lead. They'd like to back off. Some of their opponents are friends off the court. But they don't dare, because later in the season, total points or margins of victory could determine who gets into the playoffs.

They don't have any choice, in other words. Or at least, they believe they have no choice. The social environment, the system, the *unseen ground*, dictates their choices for them.

But it doesn't have to be that way. To see the influence of our cultural context, we need to look at what can happen in other cultures, other contexts. In the Canadian North, for example, stories abound of teams doing the unthinkable. When they're winning, they give their best player to the other side. Winning matters less than the game itself.

Jean Vanier knows that competition is not a universal motivation. He himself was rising fast in the Canadian Navy; he gave it up. He was headed for the priesthood; he gave that up too, to found L'Arche, an international collective of homes for seriously disabled people. He's in demand all over the world as a speaker and retreat leader; he usually shows up in a battered windbreaker apparently salvaged from a thrift shop somewhere.

To a group gathered at a retreat center in San Diego, he described another cultural pattern in the North.

In a book that came out some years ago, there was a man who claimed that if you got 25 native people from the north of Canada, 25 Indian kids, and if you said to them, "The first one who cries out the name of the capital of the United States will get a prize," the 25 will get together, and discuss it, and then they will all shout out together, "Washington." Because somewhere they know that each of them has 24 chances out of 25 of losing, but even more deeply they know that the one who wins the prize loses community. They win superiority, but they lose community.

British biologist Lyall Watson, in his book *Dark Nature*, tops even those stories. He studied the Asmat people who live in the Irian delta of Indonesian New Guinea.

Every Saturday afternoon, teams from the nearest villages meet each other in a noisy, mud-splattered, but nevertheless enthusiastic game of soccer… Despite the intense nature of the competition and the fierce struggles for possession of the ball… every game for over a decade has ended in a draw.

After a match that I watched, the referee – a recently arrived priest driven to exasperation by his umpteenth game without a decision – remonstrated with the rival captains.

"Don't you see," he said, "the object of the game is to try to *beat* the other team. Someone has to win!"

The two men looked at him with compassion, reconciled to the fact that he was young and had a lot to learn. They shook their heads firmly and said, "No, Father. That's not the way of things. Not here in Asmat. If someone wins, then someone else would have to lose – and that would never do."

Nor is this ethic limited to sporting situations. "The Asmat," Watson writes, "even handle envy with aplomb. If anyone admires or covets something, you give it to them. That puts the envious person under immediate obligation to you which can only be discharged by giving you something, or rendering you a service, of at least equal value. Envy is expensive, and, as a result, very rare in Irian."

Envy – one of the Seven Deadly Sins – is a universal emotion. It's the figure. But the response to it is not universal. Because the ground, the cultural context, is different.

Unfortunately, it's the ground that we are not aware of. That's what makes it so dangerous. Because we are not conscious of it, the ground tends to trap us. It makes us feel we have no choice.

The
Theology of
Sin

20

AUGUSTINE'S LEGACY

I didn't do it! Don't blame me! It's not my fault!

In politics, it helps to have a name near the beginning of the alphabet. If voters haven't a clue which candidate to vote for, they're more likely to mark an X for a name near the beginning of the ballot than for one near the end.

Sometimes I suspect the same principle applies in the church. A lot of the great names in the history of theological development began with A. They include Ambrose, one of the first great teachers. Arius and Athanasius squared off in bitter debate over the divinity of Christ. Other great thinkers included Anselm and Abelard. Many of these later theologians drew their inspiration from Aristotle. Or from the Islamic philosophers Avicenna or Averroës.

Some historians suggest that the most powerful intellect of them all was Aquinas. Thomas Aquinas, you may remember, solidified the previously fluid list which became the Seven Deadly Sins.

Yet I suspect we owe even more of our current understanding of sin to another man whose name began with A – Augustine.

St. Augustine's high school class would not have voted him, "The kid most likely to become a saint." They probably wouldn't even have considered him likely material for a priest. According to his own autobiographical *Confessions*, he had a libido that made today's sexual revolution look prudish. But once he recognized the sin of his own excesses, he practiced theology with the same vigor he had once pursued sex.

Augustine lived roughly three centuries after Jesus. He was born in 354 CE, and died in 430 CE. For the last 39 years of his life, he was, in the words of the *Encyclopædia Britannica*, "the dominant personality of the Western Church" and "the greatest thinker of Christian antiquity." For much of that time, he devoted his intellect to developing the doctrine of Original Sin.

Original Sin was Augustine's effort to explain how we can find ourselves trapped in a sinful situation that we had nothing to do with. It says, in effect, that it's not our fault. We're caught in something beyond our control, something that started way back with Adam and Eve. They are the ground; we are the figure.

Augustine didn't invent the doctrine of Original Sin. Its roots were certainly there in the Hebrew scriptures, which the Christian church calls the "Old" Testament. The book of Job acknowledges, peripherally, that Adam – that is, the first human – had sinned (Job 31:33). The concept comes across more clearly in the Christian New Testament. Paul, writing to the church he founded in Corinth, propounds a logic that contrasts Adam and Jesus. Paul treats mortality as the consequence – the punishment, perhaps – for Adam's sin: "For since death came through a human being, the resurrection of the dead has also come through a human being; for as all die in Adam, so will all be made alive in Christ" (1 Corinthians 15:21–22).

In other words, sin is not just a personal thing. Adam's sin casts the long shadow of mortality over everyone.

But that's never specifically spelled out in the scriptures. A lot of things aren't, of course. Many people are convinced there were "*three* wise men." In fact, the Gospel of Matthew refers to three gifts – gold, myrrh, and frankincense – but never to three givers. Nor does the Bible ever specifically refer to the Trinity. It does name each member of the Trinity separately – Father, Son, and Holy Spirit. But the Trinitarian doctrine itself was first defined by the Council of Nicaea in the fourth century after Christ, and has been a cornerstone of Christian faith since.

It took Augustine to refine the concept of Original Sin into a doctrine that has shaped our thought for 15 centuries.

OTHER POSSIBILITIES

I sometimes wonder how our world, and our faith, would be different if Augustine's theological opponents had won their argument over the nature of sin.

His main opponent was Pelagius, a British monk – a lay person, not a priest – who may have come to Rome as a law student. Ironically, both he and Augustine shared the same motivation: to enhance moral standards in the Christian community. To do it, they both retrieved, largely from Paul's letters and the other New Testament epistles, two historic ideas: free will and Original Sin. The two concepts are not necessarily incompatible – Paul saw no conflict between them, for example. But the hostility of the two men toward each other – when Pelagius first read Augustine's *Confessions*, he was reputedly horrified – forced each of them into more and more extreme positions, until compromise and consensus became impossible.

Pelagius, according to the *Concise History of the Catholic Church*, had "an intense conviction about human freedom." He believed that "man was in full control of his moral destiny."

Augustine, on the contrary, perhaps influenced by his own youth, was "profoundly impressed by the moral weakness of man and the deeply rooted character of their evil tendencies." He preached that humans "could not avoid sin without God's grace."

Augustine read the opening chapters of Genesis both literally and figuratively. Therefore Adam was both the first human, and a representative of all humans of all time. When Adam disobeyed God, all humans disobeyed God. Augustine knew nothing of genetic science, but if he had, he would have asserted that Adam's sin somehow infected his genes, like a virus, and was passed down to every unimaginably distant descendant. With that sin gene embedded in our cells, we were helpless; we could not help sinning.

Pelagius, while not denying either that Adam had existed or that he had sinned, maintained that all humans were born innocent. We were free to make choices. He was willing to admit, however, that we are influenced by the culture and society we live in. In that way, at least, we are affected by the "bad examples of Adam and his descendants." But, he insisted, we are not trapped by those "bad examples."

HEREDITY OR ENVIRONMENT

On the surface, this sounds like the old argument about nature and nurture, about genetic inheritance and environment. Do children resemble more closely their natural parents, or their adoptive parents?

One of the boys in my Scout group, long ago, was a little shrimp of a kid. His father was so tall he stooped most of the time to look less intimidating. "Jeez, Danny," I told the boy once, "when are you going to start growing as tall as your Dad?"

He looked at me in astonishment. "Didn't you know?" he demanded. "I'm adopted!"

Height was something over which he had no control. It was genetic, inherited. That's *nature* – Augustine's argument for Original Sin.

On the other hand, another son I know has no DNA in common with his stepfather. But his language, his walk, his choice of vocation, even his beard, are all uncannily like that adoptive father. I've seen some interracial adoptions – orphans from Korea, or Rwanda, or Guatemala – where the children's skin color, their hair, mark them as different. But their gestures, their accent, their unconscious habits, are the image of their new parents. Their actions and attitudes no longer bear any trace of the ethnic culture from which they once came. For them, *nurture* – their social environment – is the dominant influence.

In a family context, the line between nature and nurture is fuzzy at best. In fact, we usually recognize that it's a line that's not worth drawing. Trying to decide who influenced what just creates alienation – the last thing anyone needs in a family.

In a theological debate, it's not so easy.

A friend of ours shrugs off her shortcomings with a laugh. "I'm only human," she says easily.

"Exactly," Augustine would have agreed. "Therefore you sin. You can't help it. And therefore you suffer."

Pelagius saw that this could lead to a kind of fatalism. If the sins that enmesh me are not my fault, if there's nothing I can do to avoid being caught up in them, then why should I bother trying not to sin? It's out of my hands.

Pelagius took a more optimistic view. He insisted that God gave every person the right to choose. Every person is free to avoid sin; it's a matter of personal choice. Otherwise, God would be a vengeful tyrant punishing people for what they couldn't help doing.

Pelagius' disciples, particularly a man called Julian, pushed his ideas further. Julian argued that we do not suffer and die because God punishes us. It is not a special fate handed down to us because we have sinned. We suffer and die simply because we are mortal, like all other created creatures.

Had that viewpoint won out, it would have had enormous implications for the world.

A DIFFERENT FOCUS ENTIRELY

To use communications jargon again, Augustine's theology made humans the figure. Everything revolved around them. Julian's made humans part of the ground.

I used the term "revolved around them" deliberately. Because Augustine's view became so widely accepted that it was not for 1,000 years that anyone could challenge it. And the challenge, when it came, came not from theology but from science. A Polish astronomer and minor church official, Copernicus, used mathematics to show that the earth circled around the sun. A hundred years later, Galileo was convicted of heresy by the Inquisition for suggesting that the earth was not the center of the universe.

"Like Copernicus's revolution," writes Elaine Pagels in *Adam and Eve and the Serpent*, "Julian's threatens to dislodge humanity, psychologically and spiritually, from the center of the universe, reducing it to one species among others."

Copernicus and Galileo set in motion a change in the way we think of ourselves. Inevitably, we have been forced to realize that we are not the focus of the universe. We live on a very small planet, circling a relatively unimportant star, toward the edges of a minor galaxy. And as ecological studies continue to teach us, we humans are relatively unimportant to that planet.

Technology has given us the power to poison life all over the planet. Our greenhouse gases can change the climate of the whole world. But if all humans were to disappear instantly from the earth, our absence would have very little negative effect on other species. In fact, they would probably thrive without us. A certain number of urban raccoons and skunks would have to find a substitute for their endless supply of garbage. Pet cats and dogs would have to fend for themselves, without their life-support systems of Dog Chow or Kitty Treats. But most of the planet's life would probably welcome our absence.

On the other hand, if all the insects disappeared, life would be affected dramatically. And if all the plants disappeared, life would be impossible. Even for humans. Even with all our technology, our science, our economics, we humans could not survive without plants to create the oxygen we need.

We humans are not the crowning achievement of either evolution or God. We are not the reason for the rest of the world's existence. We are a part – an influential part, but still only a part – of a vast integrated web of life. To change the metaphor, we are a shade of color in the spectrum; we are not the rainbow.

If Pelagius and his disciples had won their theological argument 1,500 years ago, we might take our responsibilities more seriously. We might recognize that as humans, we don't have special rights, but we do have special responsibilities – if only because our technology has made us potentially the most destructive species on this earth.

WINNERS WRITE THE HISTORIES

But they didn't win. Augustine found a number of doctrinal and practical flaws in their argument.

First, it made the church irrelevant. If humans could redeem themselves from their faults by their own efforts, what was the point of baptism? Of confirmation? Of the sacraments? If people didn't need the church to mediate God's grace to them, why would they need the church at all?

Second, it wasn't biblical. It was all very well for Pelagius to claim that we bore the responsibility for our own choices. Why then should we suffer because of our ancestors' choices? Yet the Bible clearly says: "For I the Lord your God am a jealous God, punishing children for the iniquities of their parents, to the third and fourth generation..." (Exodus 20:5).

Third, it encouraged humans to think they could save themselves. That implied that humans could usurp part of the role reserved, by doctrine, for God. It also implied that humans could govern themselves – and Augustine was deeply committed to the imperial government in Rome. So his attack on Pelagius was politically expedient too.

Augustine agreed that humans had freedom of choice, once upon a time. But once humans had subjected themselves to sin by their own choice (well, by Adam's choice, but with Adam as representative of all humans), they gave up their freedom to do anything else. Having fallen by the exercise of our free will, Augustine argued, we cannot, by another exercise of will, reverse the consequences of our "fall."

Slavery, common in his time, offers a good analogy. In those days you could, to repay debts or other misdemeanors, sell yourself voluntarily into slavery. But once you became a slave, you could no longer choose to become free. Only a higher authority could free you.

We don't have slavery anymore, but alcohol addiction offers just as good an example for us. Three times a week, Alcoholics Anonymous groups meet in our church basement. At every meeting, someone stands up and says, "My name is Donald. (Or Phyllis, or Gerhardt, or whatever.) And I am an alcoholic."

The first step of the AA Twelve-Step recovery process states: "We admitted that we were powerless over alcohol, and that our lives had become unmanageable." The second is like unto it: "We came to believe that [only] a power greater than ourselves could restore us...."

The words come from Bill W., the founder of AA, in the 20th century. The spirit comes from Augustine, in North Africa, around 420 CE. We are unable to save ourselves; we have to depend on the grace of God, a "power greater than ourselves."

Augustine was a bishop; Pelagius a mere monk. Augustine was ordained; Pelagius was a lay person. Not surprisingly, the institutional church sided with Augustine. (Some church historians suggest that Augustine might have stooped low enough to swing a few deals for votes, perhaps even to buy them. Though the dispute was over theology, the decision was primarily political, and politics hasn't changed that much in 15 centuries.)

The Roman church denounced Pelagianism as heresy at a Council held in Carthage, Augustine's home turf in North Africa, in 418 CE. Six years later, another council, the Council of Orange, endorsed Augustine's views with four authoritative assertions or principles.

1. As a result of Adam's sin, both death and sin are transmitted to all his descendants.

2. Human will has been so vitiated by original sin that we can only

love God if prompted and assisted by grace.

3. Baptismal grace enables all Christians with the help of Christ to do what is necessary for salvation.

4. In every good action, even the first impulse comes from God.

As far as I know, those principles are still in force; I took them from *A Concise History of the Catholic Church,* by Thomas Bokenkotter, published by Doubleday in 1990. They entrench the underlying principles of Original Sin in the Roman Catholic Church's official *magisterium.*

DIFFERENT WORDS, SAME MEANING

The notion of Original Sin is just as prevalent today as it was in Augustine's time. We just use different words to describe it.

When Karl Menninger wrote *Whatever Happened to Sin?* he wasn't suggesting that we didn't sin anymore. Rather, he suggested, we had found ways of removing it from the realm of personal responsibility. As I noted in Chapter 4, Menninger suggested that we treat sin in the following ways.

1. As an *illness.* The illness is in control, not the person

2. As a *crime.* Responsibility shifts from individual morality to the legal enforcement.

3. As *collective irresponsibility.* The group or the "system" is responsible, not the individual.

All of these evasions, you will no doubt have noted, remove any blame from the person or the individual. They affirm, in other words, the principles of Original Sin: "It's not my fault. I couldn't help it. That's the way I was born, the way I was brought up. Don't blame me!"

In that sense, Original Sin is a cop-out.

TAKING RESPONSIBILITY FOR OURSELVES

That wasn't, I need to point out, Augustine's intention. He was simply trying to find a rational explanation for the problem of sin and suffering. Pelagius' idea had a lot of appeal. It gave people a sense of control over their lives. If things went wrong, you had only yourself to blame. But it didn't explain how people could do nothing wrong and still suffer. That's the central theme of the book of Job in the Bible – and not even Job resolves it. The story simply concludes by having God demand of Job, "What right have you got to ask such questions?"

The notion that you could be involved in doing wrong simply by belonging to a society that does wrong had not occurred to people yet. Simply by being part of a capitalist economy, a society that values money more than people, we contribute to unemployment in North America, sweatshops in Bangladesh, and deforestation in Thailand. Simply by being part of a civilization built around the automobile, we foster air pollution, sprawling suburbs, and endless shopping centers. Modern theologians describe it as systemic sin or corporate sin. I think of it as the inescapable ground that we take for granted, that we are rarely conscious of.

But whatever we call it, does it absolve us, individually, of responsibility for doing harm?

We were talking about that one day, my friend Ralph Milton and I, as we drove up the road that runs along the west side of Okanagan Lake. It's a narrow, twisting road, as contorted as a snake with severe indigestion. In places, the road is dangerous. Some corners drop off 100 feet or more, sheer to the water.

It used to be a gravel road. There weren't many accidents, because not many risked driving it. And those who did, didn't go very fast.

Then the Highways Department paved it. A few people thought they could drive a lot faster. Inevitably, a few of them went over the edge. Some were killed.

Predictably, every time there's an accident, the outcry comes, "Fix the road! Make it safe!"

But just how far can you go to protect people from themselves, we wondered as we drove along. The more you fix the curves, the more people will go faster – and find new locations to kill themselves.

Ralph – with one of those leaps of logic for which he is noted – remarked: "For years, I blamed my father for a lot of the problems I was having. One day I realized I couldn't go on blaming him for my defects. I've lived with myself a lot longer than I lived with him. So I have to take most of the responsibility for what I am."

Ralph had just overcome the limitations of the doctrine of Original Sin.

21
REVISITING EDEN

The fallacy of founding a theory on a story.

Until the age of 10, I lived in India, where my parents were missionaries. The people of India were considerably less prudish about bodily functions than the expatriate missionaries were.

My mother was so concerned about socially transmitted diseases, for example, that I wasn't allowed to sit on a toilet seat – other than in our own home – until we came to Canada. I squatted. Only my sandals ever touched the toilet seat. Given the state of toilets in Indian trains and public washrooms, her caution was probably wise.

Still, it meant that exposure to Indian customs occasionally came as a shock. One time, I was playing in the yard when some Indian people came by. There was one man, and perhaps half a dozen women.

"Hey, boy," the man said to me, "have you got a little white snake in your pants?"

I didn't know what he meant, so I ignored him. The women giggled, but said nothing.

"Take a look and see," he challenged me.

I knew very well I didn't have a snake in my pants. I would have felt it.

"I'll trade you my big brown snake for your little white snake..."

The women giggled. I felt bewildered.

"...it's a very big brown snake..."

The women giggled more.

"...they all know about it. It's much bigger than yours. You can ask them...."

The women giggled a lot more and hid their faces behind their saris.

At the time, I was still much too young to have any idea what he was talking about. In fact, I forgot about that conversation until I saw some of the Mayan ruins on Mexico's Yucatan Peninsula. The ruins at Chichen Itza, particularly, abounded in carvings of rattlesnakes. The Great Pyramid was designed with incredible precision so that at certain times of the year, the shadows cast by its terraces would look like an enormous snake descending its staircase.

We were fortunate to have, in our group of tourists, a herpetologist – the director of the reptile section of the Metropolitan Toronto Zoo. He explained that cultures all over the world have regarded the snake as a symbol of fertility.

For the first time, I realized what that man in India had been talking about. The "snake" was a male penis. What other creature, in its normal state, looks limp and flexible, but can stiffen and rear up as adders or cobras do when aroused?

And that insight gave me a whole new perception of the legend of the Garden of Eden.

THE STORY THAT EVERYONE KNOWS

I think it's worth taking another look at that story. Because it was fundamental to Augustine's concept of Original Sin. And it is still fundamental to the doctrine of "The Fall" favored by many evangelical Christians.

At a continuing education course at the Vancouver School of Theology, on Christian Spirituality and Nature, most of us took a fairly benign view of nature. Nature could be dangerous, we all admitted. But it was not normally malicious.

One woman took a different view. She rejected our teary-eyed sentimentality about nature. "We've just moved to Wisconsin," she told us. "In the summer, I have to teach my children to be afraid of tornadoes. Any storm is a potential threat. When the sirens sound, they head for the basement. And I have to teach them to be afraid of the cold in winter. It can kill them in 15 minutes."

She could not see nature as predominantly benevolent, kind, comforting. She used to, once, she said, when she lived in a suburb of New York. But in rural Wisconsin, she had come face to face with a randomness, a chaos, that had dramatically changed her perceptions.

And then, in a sudden outburst, she tied her view of nature to her theology. "Our human nature is fallen. We are a product of The Fall. We live in sin. We cannot help sinning. I believe that not just humans but the whole created order is fallen. And I don't believe that we can be healed just by changing our attitude. I don't have any faith that humans can sustain caring relationships with each other, let alone with nature. Christ is the only hope. We can only reach redemption through something beyond ourselves."

Augustine would have applauded.

It's that emphasis on "The Fall" that interests me. It presumes a particular interpretation of the Garden of Eden story.

Although the story comes at the beginning of the Bible, it is not the oldest part of scripture. That honor belongs to the stories of the Exodus, when the Hebrew people escaped from slavery in Egypt, and began to forge themselves into a new nation on the anvil of the wilderness of Sinai. As they struggled to find their way through the desert, they also struggled to find their identity. Who were they? How had they come to be what they were? And so they began to record their myths and legends about their ancestors. Their stories provided explanations for differing languages and customs, for their similarities to their enemies, for their descent into slavery.

And for their origins as humans.

One of those myths was the story of Creation. Or rather, the *two* stories of Creation. In the first story, in chapter one of Genesis, God creates the heavens and the earth, the waters and the land, the plants, the fish, the animals, and *finally* a human – in that order.

The second story, starting in chapter two, says that God created humans *first*, and then created the plants, fish, and animals as companions for the human. When they proved inadequate as life companions, God created a second human, a spouse and partner of the other sex.

The difference in order is almost irrelevant. It's simply two ways of getting to the same situation, which has both male and female humans present. But that's where the trouble starts.

We all know the rest of the story. God warned the humans not to eat a particular fruit from a tree in the garden. The humans ate it. They were changed by their act of disobedience. To punish both the man and the woman, God banished both of them from the garden – the woman to bear children in pain, the man to struggle for survival by hard work. The Bible refers to the "sweat of his brow" – a vivid image of manual labor under the broiling Middle-Eastern sun.

That is "The Fall." Humans fell from grace, from innocence, from being children in a wonderful playground to being adults cursed to work. The snake, the instigator of "the Fall," was sentenced to crawl on its belly and eat dust. The Bible doesn't indicate how the snake got around *before* The Fall.

OPEN TO MANY INTERPRETATIONS

There have been many interpretations of this seminal story. Some of the alternative scriptures of the early church, the Gnostic gospels, treated the snake as the hero. In *The Origin of Satan,* Elaine Pagels discusses such a passage from a text called the *Testimony:*

The teacher "discovers" that it reveals truth only when he reads it in reverse, recognizing that God is actually the villain, and the serpent the holy one! This teacher points out, for example, that in Genesis 2:17, God commands Adam not to eat from the fruit of the tree in the midst of Paradise, warning that "On the day that you eat of it, you shall die." But the serpent tells Eve the opposite: "You will not die, for God knows that when you eat of it your eyes will be opened, and you will be like God, knowing good and evil" (3:4,5). Who, asks the *Testimony*, told the truth? When Adam and Eve obeyed the serpent, "then the eyes of both were opened, and they knew that they were naked" (3:7). They did not die "on that day," as God had warned; instead their eyes were opened to knowledge, as the serpent had promised.

I've also seen some convoluted arguments that God gave Adam and Eve the freedom either to obey or to disobey. Free will is a mockery if you never exercise it, if you always do what someone else wants. By that standard, then, when Adam and Eve said "No" to God's command about eating the fruit, they were simultaneously saying "Yes" to God's gift of free will.

Most interpretations, however, focus on disobedience as the central theme of the story. God gave a command; the two humans chose to disobey it.

That was certainly Augustine's interpretation. But he took it further. He saw sin as infectious, like the germs my mother feared I might get from toilet seats. Adam and Eve's sin contaminated them. And because they were, according to the legend, the only two humans at the time – Augustine did not attempt to explain where the wives for Cain and Abel came from – they passed that contamination on to their descendants. All of them. Including us. That is the underlying assumption of Augustine's definition of Original Sin.

We are, therefore, not born innocent, he argued. Our lives are not a clean slate upon which to write our scripts. Augustine claimed that even at birth, part of our story has already been written on that slate. It is programmed into us, just as a brand new computer operates on programs written long before that computer was manufactured. The software of sin, Augustine insisted, runs the internal computer of every human.

Genetically, that's nonsense. Nevertheless, Augustine used it to explain our propensity to get things wrong.

A STORY ABOUT GROWING UP

Personally, I think that Augustine, and hundreds of theologians since his time, have read far too much into a fairly simple story.

I think that story is not so much about how we came to be as about how we are. It's not a scientific explanation. Like many biblical stories, it tells us our own experience. And one thing all of us have done is to grow up. We have been children, and at some point we left childhood behind.

For most of us, the transition point was our discovery of our sexuality.

When we were children, we knew there were differences between boys and girls. But they didn't matter. During the summer, I often see very young children frolicking on the shore without any clothes on. Nakedness neither excites nor upsets them. Their sex organs exist, but are irrelevant.

And then, around puberty, those same organs suddenly take over their thoughts, their jokes, their emotions. For more than a decade, I went camping with 12- to 14-year-old Boy Scouts. I discovered, to my dismay, that they had one topic of conversation. Girls. And how girls affected them. (An acquaintance described his son as The Walking Hormone!) Girls, I'm told, talk about boys the same way.

At some point, those two young persons discover sexual intercourse. And they are changed forever by that discovery. They can never go back to virginity (despite the late movie magnate Sam Goldwyn's assertion about his star Doris Day, "Hell, I knew her *before* she became a virgin!"). Nor can they ever go back to innocence.

A minister I met once used to counsel couples that once they were married, they could never go back to being unmarried. They could separate, they could divorce, they could be single, they could remarry. But they could never again be *un*married.

That is, I think, the essence of the story of Adam and Eve in the Garden of Eden. They start off as children, having no idea about the power of sex; God warns them about it, but they don't pay much attention. Then one day, they grow up. They discover sexual attraction, and they are changed by it forever. For the first time, they realize how their bodies can, even unintentionally, stimulate each other.

Their discovery had some unanticipated and painful consequences. She could become pregnant. Childbirth could be more than just painful – it could be life threatening. And if she survived childbirth, the exigencies of nursing confined her to nurturing first one, then additional, children – which forced the male into laboring alone in the fields or the forests to provide food and sustenance.

What about the serpent? As you'll have probably guessed, I think the "serpent" was simply a way of personifying the powerful persuasiveness of an erection. Although I hate to admit it, men are not very good at resisting their genital urges. In any argument between hormones and brain cells, the gonads usually win.

THE NATURE OF STORY

To describe the story of the Garden of Eden in this way is not to limit it, but to recognize what – at its heart – it tells us about. It is *not* about Original Sin, *not* about a desire to become like God, *not* about the origins of human suffering. Or if it is, those are by-products of a basic and very human story – the discovery of sexual attraction.

Now, you can make all kinds of connections to that basic story, just as you can with any human experience. When I watch politicians squabbling in the federal parliament, I may think of young children in a sandbox shouting at each other: "Did so!" "Did not!" "Did too!" Labor disputes may resemble teenagers rebelling – rightly or wrongly – against parental authority. Affirmative action programs may remind me of the spoiled brat who insists on getting his own way, or of a loving parent who gives each child the attention she deserves and needs whether or not it's a strictly equal sharing. None of those examples mean that squabbling kids in a sandbox are *about* parliamentary power, or that teenage behavior is *about* labor management relations, or that family life is *about* affirmative action programs. Those are simply connections that I make.

The Adam and Eve story invites such connections, because that "growing up" theme is reflected in so many other life experiences.

The sense of rebellion against parental authority.

The desire to blame someone else.

The loss of innocence.

The irrevocability of even casual actions.

In *An Everyday God*, I told a story from a summer spent working in the woods. At the end of a glorious day when we climbed from a rain-soaked valley to bright sunshine on a high ridge, with the whole world opening up before us, we came down to our camp.

That evening, while our supper dishes washed themselves in a burbling pool two steps beyond the fire, a helicopter came for me. After six weeks without a bath, it was time for me to have a few days off in town.

I went.

The next day, the project manager offered me an office job.

I took it.

Like people all over the world, I chose a warm bed, movies to see, a car to drive, and stores where I could buy the food I wanted.

And like people all over the world, I look back with longing at those days in Eden....

Life has always been that way. Throughout history, people have chosen hot baths and comfort over the simple natural life. They are still doing so, as underdeveloped countries opt for technology and industrial progress, in spite of the price they may have to pay in pollution and social disruption.

When any of us taste of the tree of knowledge, we learn to make choices. We establish values, set priorities, and compare benefits.

God didn't send an angel with a flaming sword to keep me from returning to Eden. God didn't have to. I made my choice.

I can't go back to Eden. None of us can. Ever.

I quote that story because it expresses *one* of the messages you can take from the story of the Garden of Eden. Once you've made your choice, rightly or wrongly, you can't go back.

But it would be a serious mistake to assume that's the *only* message it conveys. The story could also be about Augustine's Original Sin. But it could equally well convey a message about free will and individual responsibility. That was how Pelagius interpreted it. And Matthew Fox, the guru of the Creation Spirituality movement who was silenced by the Vatican for his views, took that same story as the basis for his book, *Original Blessing*. To claim that the story of Adam and Eve is *only* about Original Sin is about as ridiculous as claiming that *Winnie the Pooh* is the *only* children's story.

SETTING AUGUSTINE STRAIGHT

Obviously, I don't agree with Augustine that sin was handed down to us by Adam's actions in the Garden of Eden – entirely aside from whether there was such a person as Adam. Or Eve, for that matter – though there is apparently more scientific evidence for a universal mother than for a universal father. Augustine simply didn't understand the nature of story.

It sounds terribly presumptuous of me, a mere popularizer of theological concepts, to suggest that Augustine – a theologian and philosopher whose ideas have shaped Christian thought for 15 centuries – made a mistake. But I think he did. He didn't understand what a story is.

The meaning of a story depends on the reader or hearer. A story may illustrate a theory, understanding, or concept. It may even provide the basis for developing a theory, understanding, or concept. But it can never *prove* a theory, understanding, or concept. Because someone else, reading that same story at a different time, out of a different life experience, will derive a different message from it.

Augustine's error was not his analysis of the human situation. His observations were certainly influenced by his own life experience. But generally, they were astute and accurate. He was right about humans having a proclivity for getting things wrong. He was right that we often find ourselves enmeshed in sin. He was right that our best intentions often turn sour.

His error – in the light of the previous chapters of this book, I should probably call it his sin – lay in taking a workable interpretation for his time and place and making it absolute. In winning his dispute with Pelagius, he forced his understanding of sin onto the church as its official policy. He gave some old concepts new clothes. But when he pushed those new clothes to their limits, they flipped into a straitjacket that has constricted our thinking ever since.

PARALLEL IN THE UNIVERSE

Astronomy offers a parallel situation. Copernicus started the revolution by showing that the planets circled the sun. His mathematics predicted the movements of the planets much more accurately than previous theories could. But his theory was still slightly off, because it was based on a faulty concept. Copernicus assumed that the planets had to follow circular orbits – a legacy of Greek thought from some 20 centuries earlier.

Most other astronomers – once they accepted Copernicus' theory that the planets orbited the sun at all – blamed the inaccuracy on their observations of planetary movements, not on Copernicus' theory.

One astronomer didn't. Tycho Brahe, a Dane, spent most of his life making increasingly accurate observations of the planets. His theory was all wrong – he wanted to prove that the sun and the planets orbited about a stationary earth after all – but his observations were dead on.

Another astronomer, Johannes Kepler, trusted those observations. He spent years trying to reconcile Brahe's observations with Copernicus' calculations. He concluded that the planetary orbits could not be circular, after all. But Kepler couldn't figure out what other shape they might be. As science author James MacLachlan put it, in his book *Children of Prometheus: A History of Science and Technology,*

> After many months of laborious calculation – and some lucky breaks – he eventually realized that the shape of the orbit was an ellipse. An ellipse! All of a sudden, two thousand years of conviction that heavenly motions had to be perfectly circular came crashing down. The discrepancies between observations and predictions from the model vanished.

Over the centuries, the church has acted like the astronomers who preceded Kepler. When observation of life has conflicted with theory about life, the church has too often assumed the theory must be correct.

In the story of the Garden of Eden, Augustine found confirmation of his own experience and his observation of life. But by tying story and theory together inextricably in official church doctrine, he did us a disservice. By cementing it into the structure of the church like a cornerstone, his lofty intellectual structure led inexorably to Torquemada and the excesses of the Inquisitions in Rome and in Spain.

During his own trial by the Inquisition, Galileo offered to set up a telescope, so that his prosecutors could see what he saw in the night skies. "We do not need to see," the chief prosecutor loftily replied. "We *know.*"

Stories and theories are both based on observations. Story and theory are different ways of making sense of those observations. But it's a mistake to confuse the story with the theory.

That's the mistake Augustine made in defining Original Sin. And it has haunted us ever since.

22

SOLVING SUFFERING

*The historic assumption that pain must be punishment for sin
– ours, or someone else's.*

One Monday morning, we got a phone call to tell us that Dave and Lindy Jones' son, Allan, had died. He was 21 – young, healthy, vital. He loved physical activity. He was out playing roller hockey with friends when suddenly he slumped to the ground, unconscious. A brain aneurysm, previously undetected, had burst. His friends rushed him to hospital, where his organs were kept alive for about 24 hours.

But he was gone.

That Monday evening, I had a study group to lead. For the past month, we'd been discussing some of the great heresies of the Christian church – those dissenting notions that had come close to splitting the church: Gnosticism, Arianism, the Marcionites, the Nestorians....

When we gathered that evening, our little group didn't seem much inclined to discuss intellectual differences that had divided the church 16 centuries before. Allan's death had hit them hard. The Gnostics seemed terribly distant from this immediate tragedy.

But in fact, it turned into the most stimulating evening in the series. For we came to realize that in Allan Jones' untimely death, we had been touched personally and directly by the root of all the controversies over Christian doctrine – the struggle to integrate suffering and pain into a theology of a good God.

MAKING SENSE OF SUFFERING

The *Westminster Dictionary of the Bible* offered us one explanation for why God (portrayed in this quotation as male) permits sin and suffering:

...because the revelation of his infinite perfection is the highest conceivable good and the ultimate end of all his works... there could be no manifestation of certain of his attributes if sin were not permitted. Were there no misery, there could be no mercy shown by God; and there could be no revelation of his grace and justice if there were no sin.

Explaining suffering was not a problem when people worshipped a multitude of gods. The storm gods trashed the ripe wheat fields. Humans starved. The river god demonstrated its power by flooding the land. Cattle drowned. Whole villages were swept away. The mountain gods sent avalanches and landslides. The fire gods exploded in the forests and raced across the grasslands.

Humans suffered because they had worshipped the wrong gods. They had backed a loser. They had failed to appease a stronger god. Or, perhaps, they were just pawns – unintended victims in a higher-level feud.

Nor was suffering a problem for Zoroastrianism. Long before the time of Christ, an Iranian prophet named Zarathustra (we get Zoroaster from the Greek form of his name) expounded a dualistic theology. There was a good god, a supreme lord of creation, known in a variety of manifestations. But pitted against these were a corresponding range of evil spirits. "The events of this world," explains the *Dictionary of World Religions*, "are seen as a contest between the powers of good and evil."

But suffering was a problem for the monotheistic faiths: Judaism, Christianity, and Islam. If God was good, if God had created the universe "and saw that it was good" as the biblical book of Genesis says, where did the evil come from? Why is there pain and suffering?

THE PARADOX OF JESUS

In the early Christian church, these questions came to a head in the debate over the nature of Jesus. If Jesus was truly God in human form, why did he suffer? How could evil have enough power to nail him onto a cross, where he could die in agony, feeling alone, abandoned, having apparently failed in his ministry to show people what God wanted the world to be like?

The Marcionites – followers of a church leader named Marcion, who died around 160 CE – took a leaf from Zoroastrian doctrine. They concluded there were *two* Gods: a vengeful, legalistic God, the God of the Old Testament, and a loving God, the God of the New Testament, the one embodied in Jesus.

The Marcionites were a branch of the Gnostics, a name derived from the Greek *gnosis*, meaning to know, to have special knowledge. The Gnostics in general believed that Jesus must have been mainly *divine*. Elaine Pagels leaped to prominence with her analysis of ancient Gnostic manuscripts buried in jars near the Egyptian village of Nag Hammadi. She wrote, in *The Gnostic Gospels*,

> *The Acts of John* – one of the most famous of the gnostic texts, and one of the few discovered before Nag Hammadi… – explains that Jesus was not a human being at all; he was instead a spiritual being who adapted himself to human perception… John adds that he checked carefully for footprints, but Jesus never left any, nor did he ever blink his eyes. All of this demonstrates to John that his nature was spiritual, not human.

The Manichaeans stretched the Gnostic concept even farther. They held that the whole created world is essentially evil and sinful. Only the human soul is pure, a fleck of light in a universe of darkness. They identified Christ as pure light, pure spirit, untouched and unsoiled by a dirty world.

Other groups such as the Nestorians chose to think of Jesus as primarily *human*. He must have been, they insisted, because he suffered pain. He suffered like us, therefore he must have been like us.

The mainline Catholic Church chose to go right down the middle, with a paradox. Jesus was "fully human and fully divine." The Council of Nicaea, in 325 CE, went further. Jesus, it decreed, was not just *like* God, but of one substance with the Father – that is, *identical* to God, even while being fully human like us.

OTHER RELIGIONS, TOO

Christianity is not the only religion that has struggled with the problem of suffering. Buddhism arose from the same concerns. According to legend, Siddartha Gautama had lived a protected life inside his father's palace. When, at the age of 29, he saw death, and disease, poverty, and old age, he was so appalled that he spent the rest of his life trying to find an explanation. His explanation became, of course, the religion we call Buddhism.

Buddhism asserts, very simply, that suffering is the result of our desires. Because our desires lead us to want things, we become frustrated. Our frustration leads us to overreach our capabilities. The answer, therefore, is to get rid of our desires, to be satisfied with whatever comes to us, to be content with the day that is and nothing more. By the abolition of our desires, we will also abolish the suffering that goes with desires.

Nirvana, the ultimate goal of Buddhism, is not so much the achievement of a special state, like heaven, but the eradication of cravings – extinction of all desires, all egotism, all care about oneself.

Buddhism owes a lot to its parent, Hinduism. Western thought knows Hinduism mainly for its belief in re-incarnation, better described as *karma*.

Karma refers to the cumulative effect of acts and deeds, both in this and in previous existences. Birth and its resultant death are inevitable consequences of the karma or actions of men, explains the *Dictionary of World Religions*. When something is done, a chain of actions or reactions inevitably flows from the original deed. Thus the human being and those around him or her are caught in a never ending chain of causation.

However strange or strained you may find these explanations, they all attempt in their own way to deal with the problem of suffering. They recognize that suffering happens to all of us. Even when we haven't done anything to deserve it.

THE EQUATION OF PUNISHMENT

That apparent injustice drove Augustine to propound his doctrine of Original Sin. We suffer not because of our own sins, but because of Adam's. Eve's too. Hinduism blames it, not on an original human, but on one's previous incarnations.

All of these explanations make a common assumption: they take for granted that suffering and pain result from sin. No sin = no suffering and no pain. The equation was that simple.

The monotheistic faiths made a further assumption: God inflicted the pain as punishment for sin. Given their cultural experience, that was a reasonable expectation. If you offended the imperial authorities, you were whipped, beaten, imprisoned. Sometimes, like Jesus, you were put to death. Perhaps on a cross. Perhaps in the Roman arena, as sport for gladiators or wild animals.

Judaism, the parent of Christianity, had a strong sense of God as judge. The Hebrew prophets repeatedly charged that as the people failed God, as they weakened in their faith, God had to punish them to bring them back, to show them the error of their ways.

The concept almost certainly reflected the human understanding of the time, about the way to raise obedient children. The Book of Proverbs encapsulated it as "spare the rod and spoil the child" – a maxim much resorted to by stern (and supposedly devout) parents down through the ages. Humans have a proclivity for perceiving God in their own image.

WHEN BAD THINGS HAPPEN TO GOOD PEOPLE

The concept that sin led to punishment worked fine when bad things happened to bad people. But if bad things happened to good people, there could be only two explanations.

1. They had done something they didn't know was bad.
2. Someone else had done something bad.

Both variants are represented in the Hebrew scriptures by a pair of parables. The two books – Jonah and Job – are most likely stories told to explain problematic situations, rather than factual history.

One parable, Jonah, has the sailors on a ship caught in a storm. Everyone is suffering; everyone is at risk. The sailors conclude that they are not at fault. Therefore it must be someone else. They search the ship, and settle on Jonah. When he admits that he is running away from God (who had commanded him to go to Nineveh, a task Jonah relished about as much as a homophobic redneck would enjoy marching in a gay pride rally) they throw Jonah overboard, (where he is, as we all know, swallowed by a "great fish" and conveyed to shore). The storm, confirming the accuracy of the sailors judgment, immediately ceases.

In the second story, Job's three friends try to convince him that he must have done something dreadfully wrong to deserve his terrible fate: the loss of his sheep, his cattle, his camels, his children. If he can just find what it is and repent, the friends insist, he can be forgiven and end his punishment. Interestingly, Job never does repent. He searches his conscience and finds nothing to deserve his punishment. Finally, tormented beyond patience, he roars his outrage at God. And God responds, in effect: "Who are you to question my ways? Can you see the network of relationships that form the whole of the earth? If not, then shut up and let me run things!"

In other words, by the end, the book of Job *rejects* the idea that suffering comes as punishment for sins. Yet that message has not been heard well.

OBSERVING THE HUMAN CONDITION

Moses passed along a warning with the Ten Commandments. "For I am a jealous God," he quotes God as telling him, "punishing children for the iniquity of parents to the third and fourth generation" (Exodus 20:5). Only God had that right, however. Jewish law, formulated in Deuteronomy, specifically prohibited punishing parents for the sins of their children, or children for the sins of their parents (Deuteronomy 24:16).

(We shouldn't take the "third or fourth generation" too literally. Moses was not specifically referring to great-great-grandparents, but to one who must have died before you were born. In the Hebrew storytelling tradition, large numbers simply meant "a great many, a long time." As Herb O'Driscoll, a pretty fair storyteller himself, has commented – if you asked a Hebrew storyteller, "Were there really 70 palm trees?" he would probably reply, "Why? How many would you like?")

Your punishment, in other words, might be for the "sin" of someone you could not possibly have known about or done anything about.

Like Augustine, the ancient writers observed the human condition correctly. They saw that people suffered without having done anything to deserve it. And they were, in fact, prophetically correct in realizing that actions could have effects on later generations. We, in our time, have just begun to reach the same realization. The industrial toxins that past generations buried in supposedly safe steel drums and disposal ponds are now leaching into our water supplies. The nuclear wastes that we propose to seal in concrete could pose a threat to the next 500 generations of our descendants. The social dynamics set up two centuries ago by slavery still damage the lives of black Americans. Native people have not yet recovered from the diseases brought to their communities by white traders.

The ancient writers all took for granted, however, that their suffering was punishment. God imposed suffering on us for our own good, to bring us back into line. That was the ground that they couldn't see, the assumption they couldn't question. And so their assumption has been perpetuated, down through the ages. Martin Bucer, who lived from 1491–1551, wrote this gem:

> Since the Lord inflicts illnesses on men for the very purpose of drawing them to himself out of a lost world and moving them to seek him afresh with their whole heart... We must therefore diligently warn the sick and their companions to have no doubt that they have fallen ill because of their ingratitude to the Lord....

I saw that quoted in a church magazine in 1995. I think of it as a an example of an outdated theology. But the article cited it as a profound truth that needed to be taught to people today.

Old ideas take a long time to die.

23

MAKING A SIN OF SIN

Taking even logic to an extreme can lead to unwanted consequences.

A strange thing happened on the way to salvation. We got waylaid by sin. We took sin to an extreme, until sin flipped into the foundation of our faith.

That's a radical claim. I could probably try to justify it by citing the amount of time and energy that the Christian churches have spent haggling about sin during two millennia. I could tell you about 2,000 people burned at the stake in the Inquisition, to save them from their sins. I could go through hymnbooks, gathering statistics on how often we sing about sin. (If you want to know what people really believe, listen to what they sing, not what they say.) I could analyze the content of sermons, especially those in the churches that call themselves evangelical, conservative, or non-denominational. I could pull endless quotations from authoritative creeds and confessions.

But I won't.

I'm going to take one document, from one mainline Canadian denomination. The United Church of Canada is considered, by many, to be fairly far to the left on the theological spectrum. It doesn't, usually, make a big thing about sin. Justice, yes; sin, no.

In 1994, Dr. Thomas G. Bandy, the national staff person responsible for Congregational Mission and Evangelism, published a study paper called *Food for Faith*. He subtitled it, A Contemporary Commentary on the Statement of Faith of The United Church of Canada.

I cite this paper, not to criticize it, but simply because it hits me close to home. The United Church is my church. I attended and taught in its Sunday schools. I have attended worship in it for 50 years. I have preached in it, written for it, and received an honorary doctorate from it. I know the United Church. I do not know other churches the same way. For me to dissect any other denomination's faith statements would be presumptuous at best, foolhardy at worst.

The *Statement of Faith* on which Bandy bases his commentary dates back to 1940. It is, he notes in his preface, still the only officially approved summary of what we believe. That may surprise some, who see each new inflammatory headline as another sign of the United Church's slide from orthodoxy. The United Church did approve a creed in 1968, since amended several times. And the church has, embedded in its constitution, *The Basis of Union*, 20 Articles of Faith. Those Articles were, however, written before the United Church was actually formed in 1925. For that reason, they can't be a statement of the United Church's faith – only a summary of the faith of the denominations which merged to form the United Church.

Which leaves the *Statement of Faith* approved in 1940 by the United Church's ninth General Council as the church's only authoritative description of its theology.

FOUNDATIONAL ASSERTIONS

The *Statement of Faith* makes a series of assertions about God, Jesus, the Holy Spirit, Humanity and Our Sin, Redemption, the Church, the Ministry, the Holy Scriptures, and so on. The language is so straightforward, so unpretentious, that I had taken it for granted – which, as you may recall from previous chapters, is frequently a danger sign. I'm grateful to Thomas Bandy for unraveling some of the implications behind the assertions themselves.

Bandy's commentary is thorough. It is carefully and logically constructed. Almost to an extreme.

Thus, when he talks about God, he describes the difficulty we humans have feeling any kind of closeness to a being that is utterly different from us, utterly beyond us.

> This transcendence of God, this otherness or strangeness… is crucial to our discussion of the One God as distinct from the idolatry of many gods. If a human expression claims to fully define God, then that expression, word, feeling, or form, is idolatrous… God is beyond conceptualization, beyond proof, beyond rational demonstration.

That separation, that otherness, is resolved in Jesus. Jesus is the human face of God. Jesus overcomes the "otherness" of God by being one of us. But not *just* a human like us. Bandy says:

> We believe that Jesus is different from humanity as such, that his relation to God is by nature rather than grace… This makes Jesus the decisive window into the nature of God, and transforms Jesus from teacher and friend into Savior and Redeemer as well.

A Savior and Redeemer cannot be limited to a particular period of history. For Christians believe Jesus is the Savior of *all* people, of all times. Yet he was a real person, who lived a real life, in a real place, at a real time. Bandy disposes of the Gnostic claim that Jesus was not really one of us; "If there is any pretence about Jesus' suffering and death, then his subsequent victory and resurrection becomes equally artificial."

But if he was real for one time, then how can he still be real for our time, our world?

That conundrum is answered by the Holy Spirit, which is not limited by time or space.

Do you see what I mean when I say that Bandy builds a very logically constructed argument? Every piece connects to the next piece. Our belief in Jesus Christ, he admits, tends to be shaped by, and grow from, certain key issues left over from the doctrine of God. It should be no surprise then, that our belief in the Holy Spirit is equally shaped by, and grows from, certain key issues left over from the outline of our doctrine of Jesus Christ.

And, our belief in God requires a belief in Christ in order to be complete. Our belief in Christ requires a belief in the Holy Spirit in order to be complete.

GETTING DOWN TO SIN

Now follow me through Bandy's exploration of sin.

If sin is regarded only as a moral failure in our human decision making and action, then Christ need only be another wise human teacher or prophet... We believe, however, that sin is more radical than this. Sin holds humankind in such bondage that even if we were shown the right way, and even if we were motivated to do it, we would not be able to do so. Our human decision making is so warped that we are not able to choose the good; our human power to act is so enfeebled that we are not able to will what is right... Sin that is as radical as this requires more than a teacher. It requires a liberator and a healer. No power is greater than sin except God; therefore, God in person is required to overcome sin.

Note that term "radical sin." Bandy makes a distinction between ordinary sins, moral lapses, which we can probably fix up if we are willing to make the effort, like snaffling an extra chocolate chip cookie when no one is watching, and what he calls radical sin.

Radical sin is the kind of insidious power that turns even our best intentions into mistakes. We try to be kind, and it turns into dehumanizing charity; we try to be polite, and it turns into condescension; we try to share our benefits with others, and it turns into imperialism; we try to be good and it turns into self-righteousness and arrogance. Radical sin is our human proclivity to get it wrong; it is the sticky web of social and systemic evil in which we find ourselves caught despite our best efforts. It is Hinduism's *karma*, Lynn MacDonald's corporate sin, Augustine's Original Sin. Bandy suggests that Original Sin may be better called universal sin or inevitable sin.

"From birth we are bound and shackled in such a way that even if we wanted to do what is good, our human desires and weaknesses are such that we would inevitably fail," Bandy writes. "It is a radical alienation from God... No human being is exempt. All are sinful. It is a selfishness or pride which cannot be eradicated by human will, because it lies prior to human will."

That's "radical sin." It's beyond our control.

THE PUNCH LINE

"If radical sin is universal," Bandy concludes, "then radical grace must be universal... That grace is Jesus Christ."

Do you see what has happened here? The whole carefully constructed structure that starts with God, moves on through Jesus, the Holy Spirit, and the Trinity, turns out to have as its fulcrum, its *raison d'être*, not God but sin.

Jesus had to be, because sin already was. Since sin is universal, radical, and irresistible in human lives, God had to do something equally universal, radical, and irresistible to show that sin could be overcome.

Without that overwhelming reality of sin, Jesus would be unnecessary. God wouldn't have had to become human, someone so perfect that it could never be said by anyone, ever, that he might have deserved the punishment he received. The punishment Jesus received on the cross had to be totally unmerited, undeserved. Radical sin demands – even requires – a radical response, which was Jesus.

Lest you think I'm singling Dr. Bandy out for unfair criticism, you should realize that his is not a new interpretation. It's almost identical to the theology expounded by Anselm, Bishop of Canterbury in England around the time of the Norman Conquest of England. Karen Armstrong, in her best-selling book *A History of God,* summarizes the argument Anselm advanced about 1099:

> Sin... had always been an affront of such magnitude that atonement was necessary if God's plans for the human race were not to be completely thwarted... God's justice demanded that the debt be repaid by one who was both God and man; the magnitude of this offence meant that only the Son of God could effect our salvation, but, as a man had been responsible, the redeemer also had to be a member of the human race.

A SINFUL FOCUS ON SIN

It is because we know sin so well that we need to know Jesus.

It is because we suffer undeserved pain that we need to have a God who also suffered without deserving it.

The foundation of our theology is our knowledge of sin.

Now, I don't know whether that interpretation is right or not – and I have no doubt that many people will dispute it. But let's look at what's happened in this process. We started out with an awareness of the presence of evil. It was not dominating our lives; it did not intrude into every moment. But it did cause pain and suffering. We wanted to find an explanation for that universal experience of suffering. With the best of intentions, we developed theories that seemed to make sense. They fitted together well. They provided an integrated outlook on life – a structure of beliefs – which has proved itself meaningful to many millions of people over many centuries. It centers on God.

And unexpectedly, we find that the cause, the driving force, has somehow reversed itself somewhere along the way. In McLuhan's terms, it flipped. A structure supposedly centered on God turns out to have, at its center, our awareness of sin.

In Chapter 15, I pointed out *that any human virtue, taken to an extreme, can flip into a sin.* Good intentions can backfire.

Chapter 16 noted *we can never know precisely when something good becomes a sin.* We can only recognize what has happened in hindsight.

Chapter 17 explored the idea that *sin is something we find ourselves trapped in.* We don't choose to go that route. But once were in, we don't know how to get out.

Chapter 18 identified another factor: *sins always involve beliefs.* That's why our first reaction to the awareness of being caught in sin is shock. Disbelief. Irrational rejection.

Chapter 19 made a further point: *sin depends on us not knowing what we're doing.* The things we take for granted are most likely to trap us in sin.

The only question left is whether this focus on sin is *harmful* or not. Does it cause pain or suffering? Does it have social consequences (Chapter 3)? I can't answer that question. Only you can do that, out of your own experience.

WHEN THE OBSESSION TAKES OVER

Little wonder that television programs, when they portray religious people, tend to portray fanatics and hypocrites. Not that scriptwriters and producers go through this kind of analysis. But if they are keen observers of human nature, as Augustine was, for example, they can't help noticing that what obsesses people eventually takes them over.

So you have the cheerless village elder, committed to rooting out adultery in his community. Eventually, he finds his own desires totally driven by sex. Or the fiery reformer, bearded and brawny, committed to restoring decency to a squalid slum. He's so committed, he'll use dirty tricks to achieve his goal. Or the devout Hispanic mother, retreating regularly to her bedroom to pray in her private shrine. You can predict that by the end of the hour, she will have retreated even further into her private world, where it's okay to murder her own daughter to prevent her from sinning anymore.

Of course these are stereotypes. They're caricatures. But we have all seen them on the screen.

Northrop Frye, in his book *Divisions on a Ground*, remarked that whatever a society chooses to protect will, inevitably, come to dominate that society. Middle-class Victorian society set out to protect the delicate sensitivities of women (ignoring the fact – so obvious in hindsight – that much of their delicate sensitivity was imaginary, and more of it was caused by the tyranny of their corsets). Inevitably, said Frye, although women were isolated from the real world, the standards considered appropriate for them came to dominate all aspects of social conduct.

> Women in that society were made the focus of the social anxieties of their time: they were supposed to be the keepers of good manners, of proper speech and proper behavior. Hence the conditions set up for them subordinated them under the guise of protecting them... The result... was, of course, that society became very largely matriarchal. Women accepted the ethos which had been handed them, and imposed it on the rest of society.

In the same way, in our time, we have tried to protect children and teenagers from the harsh realities of the working world – or, at least, from the working world our parents and grandparents knew during the Depression and the war years. So we outlawed child labor. We kept young people in school longer. Guess whose images therefore dominate television programs. Or whose music fills our radio broadcasts. And whose pictures appear in our advertising. To quote Frye again:

> So there came a social system which both subordinated and protected young people, in the age group from puberty to majority, and which did with adolescence substantially what the Victorian middle-class had done with women. The result was the same, the

growth and eventual domination of society by an adolescent ethos. This ethos dominates the mass market... it dominates entertainment, and now it tends increasingly to dominate politics....

Just as our possessions can sometimes possess us, our obsessions can often obsess us. They take control.

A story describes two Buddhist monks, one older, one younger, walking along. About noon, they came to a swiftly flowing river. A young woman, pretty but slight, was afraid to cross by herself. The older monk, without hesitation, picked up the woman and carried her across to the other bank, where he left her to go on her way.

The two monks proceeded on their journey. Late in the day, the younger monk could contain his concern no longer. My father, he said, using the customary deference to an older man, how could you do that? Our vows forbid us to touch any woman. You not only touched that woman – you carried her in your arms across that river!

Yes, I carried her across the river, the older man smiled sadly. But you, my son, have carried that woman with you the whole afternoon.

The "So What?" of Sin

24
The Seven Sins Today

Applying our discoveries to the current context.

And so now we come to the crucial question, the point of this whole exercise. What burdens might we, in our North American context, be carrying with us without knowing it?

It's worth, for one last time, working back through the characteristics that identify sin.

- ✤ We take something for granted.
- ✤ It causes pain and suffering. It harms or damages someone. It has social consequences.
- ✤ We feel trapped by the situation, which doesn't seem to be of our own making.
- ✤ We resist recognizing our complicity in that harm, that damage, that suffering. It always comes as a shock.
- ✤ We never know exactly when or how good intentions turned into harmful effects.
- ✤ We realize that when we took good intentions to an extreme, they flipped into their opposite.
- ✤ We only recognize what has happened in hindsight.
- ✤ The situation involves our beliefs, our deepest convictions.

The easiest part of the process of naming the sins of our time is looking for things that harm someone or something, that cause pain and suffering. For those, you can look almost anywhere. Population pressures. Noise pollution. Global warming. Dying frogs. Industrial gases. Civil wars. Political corruption. Family breakdown. Stockpiled missiles. Young offenders. Drunken driving. Unsafe sex…

The hardest part is identifying the things we take for granted. We have to learn to look at the ground, rather than the figure. We have to learn to see what we're normally not aware of. Because as long as we dont know it's there, we can't do anything about it.

Then we can start asking the supplementary questions:

❦ Does it seem like something over which we have no control? Do we think we just have to accept it?

❦ Do we resist accepting any responsibility for it? Do we, like Pontius Pilate, attempt to wash our hands of it?

❦ Do we defend ourselves, by insisting that it had good intentions?

❦ Did we take those good intentions to an extreme? Did we make them an idol, a god?

❦ Does the cure require us to reconsider our beliefs or convictions?

If we answer yes to those questions, then I submit, we have identified a sin of our time.

At the risk of doing your thinking for you, I want to identify some of the things I see as the unexamined sins of our time. They are dangerous, I believe, precisely because they are unexamined. They have their good qualities, maybe even essential qualities. But because we don't realize where they are taking us, we follow them blindly, until they lead us into extreme positions. And then, belatedly, we discover how harmful they have become.

I don't intend to deal with these sins in detail. Each of them probably deserves a book of its own – and in some cases, someone else has already written that book. When I know of such a book, I'll recommend it for further reading. Rather than build a definitive case for each of these sins, Im simply going to sketch them loosely.

You may not think that all of these are sins, as such. Or you may have a variety of other sins to offer. I don't expect you to agree with my selection. In fact, you'll disappoint me if you do. You may even find some of my suggestions offensive. All I ask is that you apply to them the questions and principles I have outlined above.

INDIVIDUALISM

In 1995, the government of Canada passed a law that permits police to take DNA samples from suspected criminals. In much the same way as a judge issues a search warrant that allows police to examine a suspect's premises for evidence of guilt, the new legislation allows police to search a suspect's genes for evidence.

DNA is, of course, the individual blueprint for our bodies. It is even more unique – if that's possible – than our fingerprints.

Reaction to Bill C104, such as there was, tended to portray DNA testing as an infringement of privacy, of human rights. "The police," blustered one commentator, paraphrasing a former prime minister, "have no business in the *bloodstreams* of the nation."

When Pierre Trudeau announced idealistically, "The state has no business in the bedrooms of the nation," he was wrong. Sex does not always happen between consenting adults. It can also involve children and unwilling victims. The trials of Paul Bernardo and Karla Homolka showed us how sex can turn into pornography, rape, violence, and murder. Other less-than-idealistic expressions include prostitution, incest, and abuse.

When individual rights conflict with the rights of the community, something has gone wrong. Somewhere, we have gotten off the track. The current demand for victims' rights – the feeling that the justice system cares more about the rights of the criminal than those of the criminal's victims – makes vocal that sense of unease.

Robert Bellah, in *Habits of the Heart,* pointed out that in North America, the rights of the individual have been raised to an ideology. Individualism has become, perhaps, the most pervasive religion in North America. The only way we can imagine breaking away from the individualistic mindset is to become even more individualistic.

When the welfare of the community is at stake, there is no such thing as a right to privacy. A man's home is *not* his castle; he cannot always do as he wants in it. He can walk around in his boxer shorts, but he cannot commit incest. A couple can grow mold under their refrigerator, but they cannot starve their baby. He can clean his fingernails with a foot-long hunting knife, but he cannot threaten his wife with it. She can litter the living room with empty beer cans, but she cannot beat her children.

When right-wing terrorists exploded a bomb at the federal building in Oklahoma City, they demonstrated graphically the dangers of rampant individualism.

The threat to US security has never come from the left, despite Senator Joseph McCarthy's fulminations in the 1950s. Communism flowers only where a class structure exists. Not in a consumer economy, where the national dream is to become an entrepreneur and exploit everyone else. Marxism, in middle-class US, could be a means of analysis, but never a mass movement.

The real risk has always come from the right – and it has been a risk because it is so taken for granted. The agenda of the right has been clearly stated – to have less interference in their lives. What they fear above all is someone else telling them that it's not acceptable to impose their will on others, to exclude others on the basis of race or sex or creed, to bully or threaten.

Individual rights have a noble origin. Our society may not be accurately described as Christian anymore. Some speak of it as post-Christian. But as columnist Richard Gwyn has pointed out, it is certainly post-*Christian* – not post-Buddhist, post-Hindu, or post-anything else. Its cultural roots lie in Christianity. And the founding example for Christianity, the man called

Jesus of Nazareth, went out of his way to honor the value of individuals. He healed lepers, the outcasts of society. He stopped to pay attention to blind beggars. He felt, somehow, the touch of a socially ostracized woman in a crowd. He singled out for attention an elderly widow paying her temple tax.

In a society where individuals had almost no value, his was a radical corrective. A Roman soldier would probably not even receive a reprimand for raping a teenaged girl in Nazareth, say, or sticking a spear through a convicted criminal in Jerusalem. Women and children were little more than slaves. Life was brief, life was cheap, life was harsh.

But it may be that today the pendulum has swung too far. In our society, the corrective may need to go the other way.

PRIVATE PROPERTY

The second sin is like unto the first. We have elevated private ownership to a status that can no longer be challenged.

The first explorers arrived on a continent already populated by indigenous peoples. The explorers simply claimed it. In their eyes, no one owned it; therefore, they could take it.

The Canadian West was settled by homesteaders. Anyone could claim 160 acres – or whatever. Land was *supposed* to be owned. If it belonged to everybody, it belonged to nobody.

That principle still applies to mining and logging permits. We take for granted that private enterprise is entitled to make a profit from resources that used to belong to everyone. (For more discussion of this point, try David Hallman's *A Place in Creation*.)

You can tell this is a belief, largely unquestioned, by observing the reaction when the flow is reversed. Governments privatize social services and corporations exploit crown land with minimal protest. But listen to the screams when governments take over what had been private enterprise. Auto insurance, 20 years ago. Medical care, 40 years ago. When a potentially rich mine is absorbed into a provincial park.

Along the lake where I live, the issue is waterfront rights. The lakeshore is public land. But during years of benign neglect, property owners near the water built their own private docks and picnic sites. Some built fences, and put up No Trespassing signs. At least one man cut down trees in the park, to improve his view. Last year, the various governments involved reasserted their ownership of the waterfront. They imposed taxes on private docks; they required access along the beach. The property owners who had built docks or fences howled. But they never questioned their right to take over land that they did not own.

Convictions about the sanctity of private property lie, I believe, at the heart of many conflicts between citizens and corporations. Those convictions lead industries to think they can store toxic chemicals in rotting barrels on *their* property. Or logging companies to think they can harvest *their* hillside of timber any way they want. Or, at a more personal level, taxpayers to cut corners on income tax or customs declarations, convinced that they harm no one by their deception. After all, it's *their* money.

I don't deny the value of private ownership. I would not want anyone at all walking into my house, using my tools, taking my car. But that's mostly because I'm afraid they won't treat those things with care; they will damage them and discard them, and we'll both be poorer. The problem is not private ownership, but the way that private ownership excludes care for anything shared or owned in common.

When I was younger, we used to get a party together to go along the beach several times a year, to clean up the trash, a neighbor down the road commented. Of course, she added reflectively, that was when we thought it was ours. Now I guess we just leave it.

MONEY

During 1996, both the New York and the Toronto Stock Exchanges hit record highs. The Dow Jones Index soared over 5000 in the first days of the year, and kept right on going up. The TSE 300 followed. All of the big Canadian banks declared record profits.

So why, if everything's going so well, aren't we all living better than ever? Why are so many people unemployed? Why is unrest mounting?

Let me suggest a simple answer. Our economy is designed for the welfare of capital, not for the welfare of people. Economists have assumed that if capital does well, so will people. The economists assumed wrong. Capital – our investments, our money – is doing very well indeed, thank you very much. We aren't.

When I was younger, I read magazines like *Popular Science* and *Popular Mechanics.* They told me a time would come when repetitious tasks would be done by robots, when people would have vastly more leisure time to enjoy. It was supposed to be a kind of heaven on earth.

I guess that time has come. Downsizing has produced double-digit unemployment in Canada – and that doesn't include all those people who have simply quit looking for work at all. A couple of million Canadians have nothing but leisure time. Those dewy-eyed dreamers failed to ask a fundamental question, when they wrote those optimistic articles: "Who's going to pay for all this leisure time?"

Robots don't pay income taxes. They don't buy consumer goods, so they don't pay sales taxes either. They don't, in fact, make any contribution to anything except corporate profits.

What should have been a dream has turned into a nightmare. As corporations continue to down-size their work forces, in a lemming-like rush to up-size their profits, more and more jobs will be automated, and more and more humans will become redundant. Governments will have to step in, to supply the necessities of life for those who can't afford them. But fewer and fewer people will have incomes from which to pay taxes. So government revenues will continue to fall, while demands for government support escalate. Business revenues will also start to fall, as fewer people have money to spend on goods and services. That will put the squeeze on the suppliers of goods and services – who will lay off more people....

And the cycle intensifies, as governments and employers slavishly obey economic theory that favors investments over people.

This is clearly a matter of blind conviction, not of common sense. Even John Maynard Keynes, the genius who established the principles on which most modern economic theory is still based, recognized this. He once commented that practical men, who believe themselves to be quite exempt from any intellectual influences, are usually the slaves of some defunct economist. Patricia Pitcher, author of *Artists, Craftsmen, and Technocrats: the Dreams, Realities, and Illusions of Leadership,* adds her own comment: "Prophetic words. Many had become his slaves before we became Milton Friedman's. In fact, in my experience, we are adept at being slaves to all sorts of ideologies."

Capitalism has given this civilization an unparalleled standard of living. Not even Roman emperors lived as well as I do. But that standard of living has been, I suspect, an unintentional by-product. It happened to be good for capital. Now what's good for capital doesn't seem to be good for people anymore.

I'm pessimistic about the future of capitalism. I suspect we're headed into a future that will make the Great Depression of the 1930s look like a Sunday school picnic. Because this time, we'll know that it's not a temporary aberration.

The dilemma derives from a fundamental fallacy in our thinking. There is no free lunch. It doesn't matter whether a service is paid for by private dollars or government dollars – it still has to be paid for. If the government doesn't pay for medical services, you will. If the government doesn't pay building inspectors, you will – probably by massive repairs bills that could have been prevented. The pie of wealth is finite; the payment all comes from the same pot, however it may be routed.

When a company saves money by firing its workers, support has to come from somewhere else. If no one else can hire those workers, the support has to come from the common purse. Company profits come at the expense of the government's deficit. Unless that company's taxes increase, though, the equation has been distorted. Because there is no second pie to slice from.

Our governments will get deficits under control. They will hold the line on debts. They will privatize, they will cut back, and they will do what the economists command.

And we will not be any better off.

When an economy is designed around capital, capital will ultimately benefit, not people. (For more on this subject, try Linda McQuaig's book, *Shoot the Hippo*.)

HUMANS FIRST

My next choice may seem to conflict with the last. But sin doesn't have to be consistent. Nothing requires it to fit neatly into a system.

The sin is the belief that this planet exists for human benefit.

For years I kept in touch with a forester with whom I had worked one summer. He was a thoughtful man, honest, ethical in his dealings with his employees and his customers. In our last exchange of letters, he argued persuasively that if forests were not logged, they would go to waste. I suggested that would be true only if the forests' only purpose was to supply lumber for our homes and paper for our printing presses. I have not heard from him since.

Ignatius Loyola, the founder of the Roman Catholic Jesuit order, unintentionally defined this sin quite explicitly way back in the mid 1500s. In the "Principle and Foundation" of his famed *Spiritual Exercises,* he wrote: "Everything else on earth has been created for man's sake."

For centuries, we have described the earth's resources as inexhaustible. That's what we called the cod fishery off Newfoundland, the salmon run in British Columbia, the bison herds on the prairies, the great whales in the Antarctic oceans. In this century – yes, even in this decade – we have seen them all reduced to a fraction.

We have plundered these living creatures with the sublime conviction that they were put there for our use. Whaling ships took thousands of giant land tortoises from the Galápagos Islands. The tortoises could survive months without food or water – even flipped upside down and stacked like cordwood in a ship's hold. It was torture for the tortoises, but fresh meat for the sailors.

Two of the earliest stories of the Bible identify our self-centeredness.

In the story of Creation, God says to the newly formed male and female, "Be fruitful and multiply, and fill the earth and subdue it; and have dominion over the fish of the sea and the birds of the air... I have given you every plant yielding seed that is on the face of the earth..." (Genesis 1:28–29).

In the story of Noah, we read, "Every bird of the air, everything that creeps on the ground, all the fish of the sea: into your hand they are delivered. Every moving thing that lives shall be food for you; and just as I gave you the green plants, I give you everything" (Genesis 9:2ff).

On the basis of verses such as those, we have assumed an explicit right to use, abuse, consume, and destroy all that exists on the planet. But that's a selective reading. We have ignored the parallel messages: The Lord God took the man and put him in the Garden of Eden *to till it and keep it* (Genesis 2:15). God made all the other creatures, and God saw that it was good. After the flood, God describes the rainbow to Noah as the sign of the covenant that I make between me and you *and every living creature...* (Genesis 9:8–17). God does this, not just once, but *six times* within these few verses!

There is concern, today, about the depletion of fish, of forests, of wildlife. But that concern still centers on us. *Our* fishing industry. *Our* ability to breath oxygen. *Our* right to see bears or wolves in a national park.

We don't need complex scientific studies to see what's happening. A decade ago, visitors to the Adams River saw the river run red with spawning salmon. Six years ago, some pools were red. Two years ago, you had to look hard to see salmon at all.

I recall logging trucks thundering down the highway carrying three – at the most four or five – massive trunks. Today, those same trucks are loaded with toothpicks. There's nothing left but small stuff. But to hear the industry, you'd think the only issue was their jobs.

Travel writer Paul Theroux, in his book about China, *Riding the Iron Rooster*, laments the loss of many rare creatures. Their horns are ground up for aphrodisiacs, their internal organs stewed for rheumatism or high blood pressure, their flesh considered a rare and specially valued delicacy. Theroux argues, perhaps too harshly, that the Chinese have no sense of the value of endangered species. The last animal, the last fern, the last shoot, will go down with the astonished epitaph: "But it tasted good."

I don't know how correct Theroux is about the Chinese. But his analysis would also apply to many North Americans. The idea that development should cease in order to protect a small spotted owl, let alone a tree, is anathema to most people, in China or North America. Humans come first.

We have seen our planet from outer space. We know there is no other place to go, no other source from which to replace vanished species. The discovery of what might be microbes from Mars launched a lot of speculation that there might be life on another planet, but it failed to shake our delusion that we humans are the only life on this planet – or at least the only life that matters.

SYSTEMS

We have a compulsion to control things. As the realization grows that humans could be in trouble if our actions render too many other life forms extinct, so does our desire to manage and manipulate the planet. Mostly for our benefit, of course. Sometimes we also help endangered owls or marmots or salmon. But still for our benefit. We dam and divert rivers. We seed clouds to make them rain. We try to predict earthquakes and eruptions, typhoons and droughts, to minimize their effects upon us.

As part of our compulsion to control, we create systems. When the treasurer of the Episcopal Church in the USA absconded with some $2.2 million from church funds, the presiding bishop announced that this would not happen again; the church had instituted some new systems to prevent it. A warehouse manager, lamenting the incompetence of his staff, explained that he had set up systems to keep them from making more mistakes.

Systems do reduce the possibility of error. But they do it by reducing people to less than they are, or could be. Systems don't make people more honest. Or more competent. Systems start with the presumption that people are dishonest, incompetent, irresponsible, and untrustworthy. Systems, by their very nature, dehumanize people. They reduce freedom, creativity, compassion. The more rigid the system, the more each individual becomes a human robot performing preset routines. Systems deny human uniqueness; if a system is working really well, you can substitute one person for another with no loss of productivity or efficiency.

Systems put the system-maker in control; they remove control from everyone else. Listen to a sales clerk explaining why she can't accept that product for a refund, to a social worker explaining why he can't issue a food voucher, to a garbage collector explaining why he can't take away your empty paint cans.

(For a devastating critique of management and systems in business, try *Artists, Craftsman, and Technocrats*, by Patricia Pitcher.)

When parents discovered pornography and racism on the Internet, they predictably insisted that someone regulate it. It was a reasonable request. From the beginning of time, we humans have organized ourselves by some fundamental assumptions. One of those is that something or someone must be in charge. A family must have a head; a committee must have a chair; a corporation must have a board of directors. We expect someone, or something, to be in control.

For that reason, I suspect, the most common description of God is "almighty" – the one who can do anything, anytime, the one who controls everything.

The Internet threatens that understanding. Because on the Internet, no one is in control. The Internet has no source. No head. No one in charge. It doesn't even have its own technology. It simply has sites – computers on line. Knock out any of those computers and the Net will re-route itself with barely a blip. You can't pull something off the Net, because by the time you've traced it, it's already on a thousand other computers.

The Internet simply is.

And it's making more and more people uncomfortable. Because it challenges our compulsion to control.

THE QUICK FIX

When testing first identified massive ozone depletion in the upper atmosphere, scientists scrambled to find the cause. It turned out to be what we had been told were inert gases used for refrigerators and spray cans. The discovery could have changed our lifestyles. We might have reduced our dependence on air conditioning, on freezers, on aerosol everything. We didn't. Instead, we plowed enormous amounts of research into finding a slightly less hazardous substitute gas that would let us continue living as we had.

When global warming became a threat, someone seriously suggested stirring up all the oceans. They could absorb more carbon dioxide from the air. Thus we wouldn't have to do anything about our profligate burning of fossil fuels, the main source of greenhouse gases. The effect on global weather patterns, and what happened when the oceans reached their saturation point, was apparently not considered.

In the 1970s, energy consumption in both Ontario and Quebec threatened to outstrip supplies. Quebec responded with the James Bay project, flooding vast portions of the northern province. It disrupted wildlife migration and native life patterns. Ontario opted for a necklace of nuclear power generation rimming the shores of the Great Lakes. Both provinces reacted strongly against criticisms that energy conservation, recycling, and small scale generation from alternative sources could be more efficient in the long run.

We have, to summarize these examples, a fixation with quick-fix technologies. Whatever the problem, we demand fast, fast relief. If one pill will cure a headache, two will cure it quicker. If one ton of fertilizer will make a field more fertile, two tons will produce even bigger crops. This fixation has led us to dowse our lawns with herbicides instead of painfully pulling weeds, to liposuction instead of exercise or healthy diets, to political spin-doctors instead of long-term integrity.

A few decades ago, the Green Revolution was supposed to solve the world's food problems. Since then, we have had the Ethiopian famine. The soils dosed with fertilizer have been depleted. The crops have failed.

Fix is an appropriate description, for it applies equally well to the North American drug culture. No longer satisfied with the happiness that results from healthy relationships, work well done, or the beauties of nature, millions of people turn to drugs for quick and artificial highs. But again, rather than dealing with its own internal drug abuse problem, the US tried for a quick fix by invading Panama, to restrict the flow of drugs. It funded civil war in Colombia, to dethrone the drug cartels, who are themselves funded by US funds from drug users.

The quick fix does not work. But we are as addicted to it as any addict is to heroin or cocaine.

SCAPEGOATING

A news item reported that a man had sued a hospital in Florida for removing his hand. He had insisted they remove his hand. He had read, in the Bible, "If your right hand causes you to sin, cut it off and throw it away" (Matthew 5:30). His family had tried to dissuade him. So had the hospital surgeons. But he insisted. Now, handless, he had changed his mind. So he was suing the hospital for failing to try hard enough to talk him out of the surgery.

If the story weren't tragic, it would be ludicrous. But it's an extreme example of a mindset that has become endemic. Ours has become a litigious society. We have to find someone to blame. For anything that goes wrong.

What we can't accomplish through the legitimate channels, we take into our own hands. Movies like *Dirty Harry* celebrate the bitter vindictiveness of those who cannot rest until they have extracted vengeance.

The sin does not merely afflict us at a personal level. Labor and management blame each other for unrest. Political parties constantly blame their opposition for fouling up the economy. Canada blames the US for free trade agreements that have wiped out an estimated 300,000 jobs. The US blamed the Soviet Union and international communism for all its internal ills, until both the USSR and communism expired; now it blames Cuba.

The rationale for Augustine's doctrine of Original Sin has come home to roost. But we are too scientific today to blame everything on a long-dead ancestor who may only be a myth anyway. So when we find ourselves trapped in a mess not of our own making – and sometimes of our own making – we lash out at someone. Anyone. Anyone but ourselves.

I wonder, once again, how our world might be different had Pelagius won, instead of Augustine. If the dominant theology of 16 centuries had been free will and personal responsibility, rather than predestined helplessness, would we still seek scapegoats?

The original scapegoat was, literally, a goat. When the Hebrew people were wandering through the wilderness, they sacrificed animals to atone for their sins. But under certain circumstances, they could take a live goat, and confess over it all the iniquities of the people of Israel, and all their transgressions, all their sins, putting them on the head of the goat, and sending it away into the wilderness… (Leviticus 16:21).

It was not, however, an act of vengeance. The goat was not being punished. This was an act of cleansing. It allowed the people symbolically to shed their bickering and hostility, to heal wounds, to set aside the petty feuds and differences that pride would not otherwise let them forget, and to get on with living together in reasonable harmony.

That is almost the diametric opposite of what's happening today. We have become a nation of Shylocks, demanding our pound of flesh for every slight or injury. We nurse grudges. We demand restitution, not reconciliation; we want to get even, not to forgive.

The man who told us to love our enemies and to turn the other cheek would, I'm sure, be very disappointed in us.

THE SEVEN SINS TODAY

So there you have them, my Seven Deadly Sins for today. The Seven is both fortunate, and fortuitous. I could just as easily have limited the number to five, or increased it to 14. Indeed, if you were to challenge me about these contemporary sins a year from now, I might well come up with a decidedly different list.

The number seven has no more significance now than it had centuries ago, but its a nice round number – well, all right, an angular number – that rounds out the book. I started with the historic Seven Deadly Sins; I conclude it with a contemporary Seven.

You can probably, with a little bit of trial and error, match up the two lists, more or less. That doesn't prove that my list is right, or even comprehensive. It demonstrates only the wisdom of those who devised the original list. Probably *any* list that you or I could devise would correspond, in one way or another, to those seven pervasive human character traits that we still call the Seven Deadly Sins.

25
ENOUGH!

Learning to live with the ambiguity that falls somewhere between the extremes.

Our daughter Sharon has absorbed hours of unsolicited advice from her parents. When she feels just about drowned by it, she cocks her head to one side, flaps her eyelashes, and asks innocently, "So, what's your point, Dad?"

It's a good question. A media guru asked the same question in my first job, when I was learning to write radio commercials. "You gave them all the reasons for having a second refrigerator in their houses," the guru told me. "But you never told them to go and buy it!"

"Isn't that obvious?" I protested.

"The answer is never obvious," he glowered down at me. "People won't make the effort to figure things out. You have to tell them."

He gave me a formula to follow in writing. The final item in that formula asked, "So what?"

SO WHAT?

So I've come to the final chapter in this book. So what?

We've learned a lot about sin. So what?

What difference does all this make to our lives, and our living? What difference could it, or should it, make?

At the risk of stating the obvious, I think there are three implications from this book.

1. We need, once again, to name harmful extremes as sin when we see them.
2. We need to trust ourselves to live with the ambiguities between the extremes.
3. We need to learn when to cry enough.

IF THE SHOE FITS

Sin matters. But in this time of transition, when so many of the old values come under question, and so many of the old questions are treated as irrelevant, even those who know that sin matters have grown leery of pointing fingers and saying, That's a sin!

We need to name the sins we see. By refraining from identifying sin as sin, we do no favor to ourselves or to the sinners. And remember, those sinners may be ourselves as well as others. By refraining from naming the sin as sin – from fear, from embarrassment, from a desire not to offend – we progressively train ourselves to accept the unacceptable. We allow people to persuade themselves that they really haven't done anything wrong, after all.

We need to stress the importance of motivation in sin. In our region of British Columbia, recently, there has been some controversy over bear hunting. Should it, or should it not, be allowed? The debate quickly identifies two extreme positions. One describes bears as "gorgeous, magnificent creatures." The other sees any restrictions as "just another shoe in the door toward taking away my right to hunt anything." Both are direct quotations from persons who phoned the CBC's morning program. In between fell comments that talked about "wildlife management," "wildlife preservation," and "harvesting." Only one person, that I heard, asked the crucial question: Why does a hunter *want* to go out and kill a bear in the wild?

We need to emphasize that sin shows up in patterns, not necessarily in single acts. To continue with the hunting illustration, it's certainly not a sin to shoot a bear that's threatening your home, your property, your family, or yourself. Nor is it a sin to shoot a bear, a moose, a rabbit, for food. But it may well be a sin if the primary motivation is simply to kill – to use a high-powered weapon to demonstrate dominance over some other creature, large or small.

Canadian native people could teach us much about motivation, if we who come from white and European origins were not still so preoccupied with demonstrating the dominance of our culture over theirs. A Haida native, John G. Williams, sent this letter to *pmc: the Practice of Ministry in Canada.*

> As far back as I can remember, our Elders impressed on us the vital importance of treating every part of the Creation as being as important as ourselves. We were taught that every living creature has its own place in nature, and if we destroy it wantonly, we are lessening our own resources for life.
>
> It was forbidden to kill any creature unless it was required for food. When the first explorers and traders arrived, they reported in their journals that "Natives prayed to the animals they killed for food, and when women were to take cedar bark to make baskets, hats, mats, or clothing, they prayed to them first." They and the first missionaries called this "animism."
>
> The truth is that when hunters killed animals for food, they thanked the Creator for this gift of life. After this, protocol demanded an apology to the creature killed, and then it was thanked for giving up its life to provide food for the hunter and his family.
>
> Nothing was done without prayer to the Creator. All life was sacred. The Creator told our ancestors, "You will have everything you need, but if you are too greedy, there will be no more, and it will not be created again."

So it is that for 500 years, our people have tried to tell the new-comers that the earth and the creatures created with us must be protected.

I'm not convinced that the native way made any difference to a salmon with a gaff hooked through its belly, or an elk with an arrow through its neck. Nor am I sure that native people always followed their own prin-ciples. I fear that in many instances, the power of the gun and the leg-hold trap may have seduced their good intentions. But as an ethic, the native tradition holds up far better, I believe, than killing for the sake of killing.

We need to be clear, in naming sins, that they may have good inten-tions. There is nothing wrong, and a lot that's laudable, in trying to bal-ance budgets and reduce deficits. But even the best of intentions, pur-sued blindly and slavishly, can be subverted into sin.

Finally, we need to recognize that when we try to identify sin, we can only recognize the extremes. It's important, therefore, when we start talking about sin, to acknowledge that we are talking about *extremes*. And it is probably *only* on the extremes that we will achieve agreement.

THE GOLDILOCKS EFFECT

We need, therefore, to learn to live with the ambiguities between the extremes.

To insist on black-and-white distinctions is itself an attempt to push questions to an extreme. In last year's municipal elections in Kelowna, our nearest city, a group calling themselves the Christian Coalition circu-lated a questionnaire to candidates. It offered only two options for re-sponses: Yes or No. One question asked if the candidates favor public funds being used to pay for abortions. A simple answer denies the com-plexity of the issue. Is abortion wrong only if it's paid for out of public funds? Does opposition to abortion mean setting aside compassion for the victim of rape? For the wayward daughter you still love?

We need to look for Aristotle's Golden Mean that lies between rigid distinctions. At the same time, we need to be wary of making a Golden Calf out of compromise. The best course may well fall somewhere in the middle – but it is not necessarily achieved by I'll give up this, if you'll give up that. Marriage counseling has taught us – or should have taught us – that when wife and husband try to get along by giving up their differences, the relationship soon spirals downward toward divorce. Marriage is healthy when two people celebrate and build on their differences, to enhance and enrich both lives.

We need to remember that the healthy Golden Mean may be difficult to define. When I was young, all the salt we bought was iodized. It had a small amount of iodine added to it. Now, on the one hand, iodine is a poison. It was used as a disinfectant for wounds and scrapes, because it destroyed bacteria and unwelcome germs. Unfortunately, it also destroyed living body cells – that's why it was so painful, and why it's been superseded by more selective disinfectants. But it still has uses. When Joan and I traveled to parts of South America not noted for water purity, the doctor at the travel clinic supplied us with a filter that used iodine to sterilize water passing through it.

On the other hand, a shortage of iodine in the local water or food can cause goiters, an abnormal swelling of the thyroid gland. Adding minute quantities of iodine to table salt reduced or prevented many goiters.

The key is to find the amount that's just right.

That's the message of the story of Goldilocks. Goldilocks visited the house of the Three Bears. She sampled their porridge, and found some of it too hot, and some of it too cold, and some of it just right. She sampled their chairs, and found one too big, and one too small, and one just right. She lay down in the beds, and found one too hard, and one too soft, and one just right.

British biologist Lyall Watson takes that story as a theme for survival. Nature, he suggests, has its own way of finding a biological equilibrium that is just right. If there are too few rabbits, the wolf population will be affected; the reduction in wolves (along with other factors) will allow the rabbit population to increase again. If there are too many locusts, the wheat harvests will be decimated, leaving less food to nourish the locusts, lowering their levels again.

The Goldilocks effect is less easy to define in ethical issues. But I believe it is just as applicable. And I believe that we, like Goldilocks, have some instinctive understandings of what just right is. We get into trouble only when we try to establish rigid definitions.

One of the paradoxes that the ancient Greeks delighted in illustrates the point. "Is a man bald if he has just one hair on his head?" it asked.

"Of course," comes the obvious answer.

"Well, then, is he still bald if he has two hairs on his head?"

"Yes."

"And suppose he has one more hair on his head?" continues the discourse.

The point is that there is no single point at which one more hair will change baldness to a full head of hair. Both descriptions are of extremes. Yet we trust ourselves to know the difference between the two.

I think we seek that just right level in our religious rituals.

Take baptism, that almost universal Christian sacrament, as an example. The central symbol is water. We all know the risks of its two extremes. Too little water in our lives, and we perish, agonizingly, of dehydration. Too much, and we drown.

We recognize both those extremes intuitively in baptism. I was, for some years, a member of a committee of the United Church of Canada trying to develop a liturgy for baptism and reaffirmation of faith that was harmonious with a growing ecumenical consensus among churches. We spent hours at each meeting, over a period of years, trying to find words that could acceptably expound our understanding of the rite and sacrament. Finally the late David Newman exploded with frustration: "Why don't we just get on with it and pour the damn water!"

While some might quibble with his choice of adjectives, his intent was clear – the symbol said more than any number of words.

In a traditional baptism, people are held under water. The action dramatizes drowning, death to an old way of life. When they rise again out of the waters, they are wet, like newborn infants freshly released from the waters of the womb; like those infants, they are beginning a new life. The imagery holds – and is stressed in the wording of the promises made by the candidates for baptism or by their parents, in infant baptisms – whether the baptism takes place by full immersion or by symbolic sprinkling.

Intuitively, we know that the volume of water has to be "just right" – neither too much nor too little. The actual amount varies according to denominational practices – but no denomination requires dropping the candidate overboard at sea, and no denomination dispenses with water entirely.

The problem is to know just what that "just right" level is in increasingly complex situations. In this book, I suggest that we can never know it exactly. We need to be content with that. We cannot define it, because to do so is itself to take precision to an extreme. Rather, we will have to be tolerant of a certain level of uncertainty. Of ambiguity.

Further, we need to trust each other within that ambiguity. We need the confidence to believe that most of those we deal with have good intentions. When we find those good intentions, we need to celebrate them. (Obviously, I'm not talking here about psychopathic serial killers or unique situations, but about those persons we encounter most of our everyday lives.)

Once again, an old Greek paradox helps to illustrate the point. (The Greeks loved these mind-games.) A Cretan, a citizen of Crete, says: "All Cretans are liars."

Now, if he's telling the absolute truth, then he himself, as a Cretan, must be lying, which means that some Cretans must, sometimes, tell the truth.

But if he's lying, that is, if some Cretans do occasionally tell the truth, then he confirms the truth of his own assertion, which means he himself is telling the truth in his lie.

Do you see the tangle this gets into? You could go on and on unraveling the ramifications forever.

But in fact, none of us has any trouble understanding the simple assertion. We know what it means. It tells us to be careful of what we hear, what we believe. Fair enough. That's good advice, in Crete or anywhere else. The problem arises only when we take that simple assertion and push it to its limits. When we treat it as an absolute. When we take it to an extreme.

KNOWING WHEN TO QUIT

The problem, to continue that thread, is that we have an inherent predisposition for taking things to extremes. We do not seem to know when to say "enough."

I worked with an editor who quit eating veal many years ago. Her father was a dairy farmer. She was brought up eating beef. She had no objection, in principle, to eating red meat. But she objected to eating veal, because the normal life of a calf was distorted to deny it any development of muscle, to reduce blood levels to near anemia, all so that humans could enjoy near-white, near-grainless, meat.

Pâté de foie is considered a delicacy. It is, in brutal simplicity, the livers of geese that have been force fed until their livers are enlarged, distorted.

Long ago, human beings discovered that they could harness the power of a stream to drive a mill wheel to obtain mechanical power, and eventually, to drive turbines that provided electrical power. Soon, they discovered that by restricting the flow of a stream, by building a small dam or weir, they could enhance the power available from that water.

Small dams did little damage to the ecology of streams. They may even have enhanced it, as beaver dams often enhanced the ability of that watershed to retain water, to meter it out progressively during the year rather than losing most of it during a single massive spring runoff.

But dams did not stay small. We built bigger and bigger dams, flooding more and more land, until building dams almost became the reason for existence of organizations like the Tennessee Valley Authority in the US. In my part of the country, in the province of British Columbia, where only some 3 percent of the total land area is level enough to be arable, a dam drowned the rich agricultural land of the Arrow Lakes. The people lost their farms, their homes, their history. The government gained long-term sales of electricity to the United States – even though, in 1994, some of that electricity was used to put on sound and light displays at Grand Coulee dam further downstream while water levels in Canada fell so low that people could walk out around their former homes, drowned for 40 years.

We simply don't know when to say "enough."

Anorexia is the inability to know when to quit dieting; obesity, usually the inability to know when to quit eating. Politicians get into trouble because they don't know when to shut up. Alcoholics have to have one more drink. Thieves get nailed because they try one more heist. Civil wars rage on because each faction wants a bit more territory. Successful firms keep jacking up their margin of profit.

We persist in pushing things to extremes. We're not content to live with an approximation of just right. We don't know when to say enough.

Shakespeare got it wrong. He had MacBeth say:

Lay on, MacDuff
And cursed be he that first doth cry, "Enough!"

Our curse is not that we quit too easily. It's that we seem incapable of learning when to cry "enough."

BIBLIOGRAPHY

Armstrong, Karen. *A History of God.* New York: Ballentine, 1993

Bibby, Reginald W. *There's Got To Be More: Connecting Churches and Canadians.* Winfield, BC: Wood Lake Books, 1995

Cousins, Norman. *Albert Schweitzer's Mission: Healing and Peace.* New York and London: W. W. Norton and Co. (Penguin in Canada), 1985

Crim, Keith, ed. *The Perennial Dictionary of World Religions.* San Francisco: Harper and Row, 1981

Frye, Northrop. *Divisions on a Ground: Essays on Canadian Culture.* Toronto: Anansi, 1982

Gehman, Snyder, ed. *The New Westminster Dictionary of the Bible.* Philadelphia: Westminster, 1970

Gleason, Allan. *Encounters with the Bible.* Winfield, BC: Wood Lake Books, 1991

Hallman, David. *A Place in Creation: Ecological Visions in Science, Religion, and Economics.* Toronto: United Church Publishing House, 1992

McLachlan, James. *Children of Prometheus; a History of Science and Technology.* Toronto: Wall and Emerson, 1989

McLuhan, Eric, Marshall McLuhan. *Laws of Media: The New Science.* Toronto: University of Toronto Press, 1988

Menninger, Karl. *Whatever Became of Sin?* New York: Hawthorn Books, 1973

Pagels, Elaine. *Adam and Eve and the Serpent.* New York: Random House, 1988

—. *The Gnostic Gospels.* New York: Random House, Vintage Books, 1981

—. *The Origin of Satan.* New York: Random House, 1995

Pitcher, Patricia. *Artists, Craftsmen, and Technocrats: The Dreams, Realities, and Illusions of Leadership.* Toronto: Stoddart, 1996

Posterski, Donald C. *True to You: Living Our Faith in Our Multi-minded World.* Winfield, BC: Wood Lake Books, 1995

Taylor, James. *An Everyday God.* Winfield, BC: Wood Lake Books, 1981

Vanier, Jean. *Healing our Brokenness.* 6 audiotapes of a retreat in San Diego. Mahwah, NJ: Paulist Press, 1990

Watson, Lyall. *Dark Nature: A Natural History of Evil.* London: Hodder and Stoughton, 1995